"Adam Zulawnik's book presents an original and innovative approach to the possibilities of applying a new methodology based on the open source program Great Manga Application Onidzuka (GMAO) to the process of translation of a Japanese graphic novel (but potentially to any multimodal text). The research paths that this methodology opens up are multifarious, contributing originally to the theory and the practice of multimodal translation with both didactic and political implications. The political role of the translator is actually seldom endorsed nowadays and still goes against any editorial guideline from any form of patronage (publishing houses, distribution companies etc.). Well-rooted in important previous studies on the topic (Mona Baker, Lawrence Venuti etc.), the author's work highlights how politically charged texts can and should have a fundamental pedagogical function, encouraging the translator to assume a braver political stance. And in doing so, Zulawnik is brave indeed."

– Prof. Irene Ranzato, Researcher and lecturer in English language and translation, Sapienza University of Rome

Translating Controversial Texts in East Asian Contexts

Zulawnik focuses on the broad concept of 'controversy' and issues pertaining to the translation of politically and historically controversial texts in East Asia.

The research methodology is exemplified through a case study in the form of the author's translation of the best-selling Japanese graphic novel (manga) *Manga Kenkanryū* (*Hate Hallyu: The Comic*) by Sharin Yamano (2005), a work that has been problematised as an attack on South Korean culture and the Korean Wave. Issues analysed and discussed in the research include translation risk, ethics, a detailed methodology for the translation of so-called controversial texts exemplified through numerous thematically divided examples from the translation of the chosen Japanese text, as well as examples from a Korean language equivalent (*Manhwa Hyeomillyu – Hate Japanese Wave*), and definition and contextualisation of the concept of 'controversy'. There has been limited research in the field of translation studies, which seeks to exemplify potential pragmatic approaches for the translation of politically-charged texts, particularly in multi-modal texts such as the graphic novel.

It is hoped that Zulawnik's research will serve both as a valuable source when examining South Korea–Japan relations and a theoretical and methodological base for further research and the development of an online augmented translation space with devices specifically suited for the translation of multi-modal texts such as – but not limited to – graphic novels and visual encyclopaedias.

Adam Zulawnik is a researcher and teaching associate/coordinator in Korean Studies at the Asia Institute, University of Melbourne and a founding member of the program. He was previously an Academy of Korean Studies Postdoctoral Research Fellow at Monash University, where he completed his PhD in translation studies and published his first co-authored book, *Interviews with North Korean Defectors: from Kim Shin-jo to Thae Yong-ho* (Routledge, 2021). His current research focuses on translation from the Korean and Japanese languages in political and historical settings and the development of a textbook about the history of the Korean Wave titled: *The History of Hallyu: from the Kim Sisters to BTS* (currently under contract with Routledge).

Routledge Advances in Translation and Interpreting Studies

Lifestyle Politics in Translation
The Shaping and Re-Shaping of Ideological Discourse
By M. Cristina Caimotto and Rachele Raus

Reframing Translators, Translators as Reframers
Edited by Dominique Faria, Marta Pacheco Pinto, and Joana Moura

Transfiction and Bordering Approaches to Theorizing Translation
Essays in Dialogue with the Work of Rosemary Arrojo
Edited by D.M Spitzer and Paulo Oliveira

Translating Controversial Texts in East Asian Contexts
A Methodology for the Translation of 'Controversy'
Adam Zulawnik

Using Technologies for Creative-Text Translation
Edited by James Hadley, Kristiina Taivalkoski-Shilov, Carlos da Silva Cardoso Teixeira, and Antonio Toral

Relevance Theory in Translation and Interpreting
A Cognitive-Pragmatic Approach
Fabrizio Gallai

Towards a Feminist Translator Studies
Intersectional Activism in Translation and Publishing
Helen Vassallo

For more information about this series, please visit www.routledge.com/ Routledge-Advances-in-Translation-and-Interpreting-Studies/book-series/RTS

Translating Controversial Texts in East Asian Contexts

A Methodology for the Translation of 'Controversy'

Adam Zulawnik

Routledge
Taylor & Francis Group

LONDON AND NEW YORK

This work was supported by the Core University Program for Korean Studies through the Ministry of Education of the Republic of Korea and Korean Studies Promotion Service of the Academy of Korean Studies (AKS-2017-OLU-2250002).

First published 2023
by Routledge
4 Park Square, Milton Park, Abingdon, Oxon OX14 4RN

and by Routledge
605 Third Avenue, New York, NY 10158

Routledge is an imprint of the Taylor & Francis Group, an Informa business

British Library Cataloguing-in-Publication Data
A catalogue record for this book is available from the British Library

Library of Congress Cataloguing-in-Publication Data
A catalog record has been requested for this book

ISBN: 978-0-367-76622-1 (hbk)
ISBN: 978-0-367-76624-5 (pbk)
ISBN: 978-1-003-16779-2 (ebk)

DOI: 10.4324/9781003167792

Typeset in Times New Roman
by Apex CoVantage, LLC

To my beloved wife Kaori and children – so that your lives are 'controversy free'.

Contents

Figures

Tables

Acknowledgments

It has been exactly a decade since I first set out on my journey into the world of translation theory and 'controversy'. Many things have changed since I first embarked on my journey as an honours student – just having arrived in Melbourne, Australia from New Zealand. We now find ourselves amidst a pandemic, dealing with the uncertainties of a future co-existing with COVID-19. And yet, many things have also remained the same – both the good and the bad. Japan-Korea (or Korea-Japan . . . I still cannot decide) relations have remained unchanged if not worse than back in 2012. We continue to grapple with North Korea. Hallyu (the Korean Wave) has continued to expand globally with *chimaek* (Korean chicken and beer) available almost everywhere, and K-Pop tunes, such as that of BTS, may be heard on local radio stations even here down-under. As if to say something, we have even seen a limited edition BTS set at McDonalds.

It has been a truly 'controversial' decade. We have lived through a Trump presidency, TikTok, 5G, and debates about vaccination. War in Ukraine, South East Asia, and a host of environmental issues. My very own existence has not strayed from the theme of controversy either. In 2021, alongside Lim Il, I published my first co-authored book: *Interviews with North Korean Defectors: from Kim Shin-jo to Thae Yonh-go* (Routledge, 2021), a tribute to North Korean defector-residents in South Korea. The work was published with support from an Academy of Korean Studies university core grant at Monash University (I was an Academy of Korean Studies postdoc from 2019–2021). My family expanded and I remarried. I briefly became an 'independent' academic, and, even whilst writing, I am a Centrelink pensioner, living day-to-day. I was fortunate to secure a new role at the University of Melbourne (Korean Studies) commencing in a few weeks' time.

In spite of all that I have been through, I am happy to be alive and delighted to have the opportunity to finally publish my work. I am also thankful for those around me (as well as those who have since passed) for always believing in me. I want to thank my PhD supervisors, Associate Professor Beatrice

Trefalt (hello from Darth Vader!) and Associate Professor Jeremy Breaden for all of the effort they put into guiding me between 2013–2018 whilst I was working on my thesis from which this book has stemmed. I appreciate the sea of red I was met with each time I went over my drafts, and I miss our meetings. I want to thank my postdoctoral supervisor Associate Professor Andrew David Jackson for his support during my two-year fellowship. You did all that was in your power to help me on my journey. I also thank all of my colleagues at Monash University, particularly Dr Shani Tobias who pushed my honours project through when it was initially met with opposition due to its 'controversial nature'. Many thanks to Dr Lucien Brown and Dr Josie Sohn, my colleagues in Korean Studies at Monash for many good times and laughs over the years. Thank you to all of my wonderful students at Monash, the University of Sydney, and Australian National University – you inspire me every day. I must also thank my wonderful colleague Associate Professor Jay Song at the Asia Institute, University of Melbourne, for much needed support and guidance in most recent times.

I would like to thank my family for all of the support I have received over the last decade. My parents, Anna and Mirosław – you are the best parents in the world and I will always think of you as my *tatuś* and *mamuśia* (and be your *Adaś*)! I want to thank my grandparents for always loving and cherishing me. My paternal *babćia* and *dziadzio* sadly passed away within a year of each other during the pandemic but will always remain deep in my heart and memories. Thank you to my grandfather Adam Piekarski and his inspirational anecdotes about risk management during the Cold War. I always keep white bed linen nearby for that worst-case scenario! Thank you to my beautiful wife Kaori and my adorable children: Joseph, Julia, Jimi, Kohana, and little AJ. Your patience and understanding never cease to amaze me. I may not always be present 'up there', but you are always in my heart and I love you beyond words.

Finally, I would like to thank Mr Yamano Sharin for allowing me to use images from his manga and all of the editors at Routledge, particularly Katie Peace, Simon Bates, and Shubhayan Chakrabarti, for always believing in me and seeing three book contracts through to signing and more on the way.

On a humid January night in Springvale,
Adam Zulawnik

Note on Romanisation

When translating names, the choice was made to provide the most popular Romanisation available or used within the source document. In cases where a popular Romanisation was unavailable, the choice was made to use 'Hepburn Romanisation' and 'Revised Romanisation of Korean' for Japanese and Korean, respectively. All translations from Japanese and Korean have been done by me unless stated otherwise.

1 Introduction

My grandfather Adam, a former sociologist and government official in Communist Poland, always reiterates an amusing anecdote regarding the reality of risk management in extreme situations where one may be met with mortal risk. When asked about the Cold War, my grandfather recounts "when schools and government offices practiced drills for potential nuclear attacks, we would always say that the ideal procedure to follow during such an emergency was to: 1) quickly wrap oneself in some white bedsheets 2) get down low on the floor 3) slowly proceed to crawl towards the nearest cemetery." I always found the anecdote funny and it became a running joke in the family when talking about risk management and the "best thing to do" to prepare oneself for the worst. The profound nature of this wisdom imparted upon me by my dear grandfather – what the quote really meant in terms of the realities of what can be done in some situations – took on new meaning when I began combining my passions of Japanese and Korean language with translation and historical investigation during my honour's year and doctoral research at Monash University. I became fascinated by the 'controversial' nature of Japan-Korea (or Korea-Japan. . .) relations. The fact that almost every facet of this 'pairing' was riddled with traps for the uninitiated. I soon discovered the many difficulties of being a Koreanist *and* Japanologist. It was as though one had to choose the chicken or the fish on a long-haul flight. You cannot have both and either or can result in trouble. If you do somehow manage to get both . . . well, you will end up in quite some trouble down the track. Japan-Korea relations, as I discuss early on in my book, are fraught with historical and political controversies. Mentioning to a Koreanist (or Japanologist) that I am also the 'other' has, more often than not, resulted in bitter smiles, followed by either difficult questions regarding my stance on key matters or total avoidance.

And so, I have grown accustomed to 'controversy'. When asked about my political stance, I will often reply: "I am a little pro-Korea, a little pro-Japan, and 100% Adam". Perhaps it is my upbringing. A 1.5 generation

DOI: 10.4324/9781003167792-1

Australasian (having lived decades in New Zealand and Australia) who left Poland with his parents at a young age, I have spent much of my life moving to and from. I am the citizen of three nations but find it hard to completely identify with one set 'place'. In fact, I find places technically 'foreign' to me, such as Korea and Japan, in many ways more familiar than, for example, Poland. Growing up in an immigrant household I have experienced my fair share of 'national pride' and 'patriotism', both which I have come to detest. The idea of 'nation' never made sense to me. I do not feel that I am completely a Pole, Kiwi, or Aussie. This has had a big impact on my academic activities and mindset when looking at Japan-Korea relations, as although I love both cultures, I cannot stand nationalistic sentiments, wherever they may be on the political spectrum. I simply cannot get into them. And so, I am myself seen as somewhat 'controversial'.

Thus, 'controversy', a negatively charged term and the focus of my work in recent years, is just as much a key concept in this book as it is in our everyday human existence. 'Controversy' is a term that is outside of the reach of most adolescents and their vocabularies, and yet the concept is universal to our experience. Without 'controversy' civilization and culture would undoubtedly make little headway. New ideas and concepts, regardless of intention, may be perceived as 'controversial' at any point in time, as though part of some cruel wheel of fortune. Regardless of what may have been the case at the time of inception of any given concept, much of what was once 'controversial' is simply not so today. Whether in reference to the practice of hand washing, mask wearing, the songs of the Beatles, or gender equality, 'once controversial' carries an almost nostalgic or even naïve air to it. That is, of course, not to fall into the trap of extreme relativism and profess that *all things* controversial are justifiable and, one day, shall become accepted or commonplace.

2 Navigating 'Controversial' Translation

In this project, I explore the issues that surround the translation of controversial and multi-modal texts by translating a volume of the Japanese graphic novel *Manga Kenkanryū* (*Hate Hallyu: The Comic*) by Yamano Sharin (Yamano, 2005). An important facet of this project is the medium of the text selected for translation as it exemplifies a newly proposed translation methodology utilising the open-source program Great Manga Application Onidzuka (GMAO). Format-specific issues include translating in a space-constrained environment, translating contextually complex multi-modal elements such as visual metaphors, as well as pertinent ethical issues, such as text choice and translator 'neutrality'. *Manga*, also known as *manhwa* (Korean), and *manhua* (Chinese), are an Asian adaptation of the "comic" or graphic novel. *Manga* are a combination of popular Edo period art forms and the traditional Western comic, which was introduced post-World War II, but they have since surpassed their predecessors in global popularity. In Japan, manga now account for 40% of all printed material (Pilcher & Brooks, 2005, as cited in Zanettin, 2008, p. 4). Although academic discussion about the translation of comics has been limited thus far, there is a steadily growing range of literature on *manga* translation (e.g., O'Hagan, 2006; Zanettin, 2008; Pasfield-Neofitou & Sell, 2016). Part of this project aims to address issues relating to the translation of *manga*, doing so through the use of technology-assisted strategies.

In the process of translating *Manga Kenkanryū*, I propose a methodology for the translation of politically charged texts for pedagogical purposes which, at the same time, tackles the problem of translator and translation invisibility. I argue that translations of politically charged texts have a specific pedagogical purpose because they exemplify, in ways that cannot be replicated elsewhere, the nature of debate that is intercultural, inter-lingual, and historically and politically bound. The fact that my project translates multi-modal media, in this case a *manga*, allows me to highlight in precise ways the interaction of the historical, political, and cultural on the text and

DOI: 10.4324/9781003167792-2

the nature of translation of such texts. Such an endeavour, however, endows the translator with an unequivocally political role, and therefore, I argue here, translation should be conducted following certain guidelines, placing the translator and their decisions in full view of the reader. In essence, the translator of a project such as this should be seen at work, countering the outdated assumption that translators are passive conduits or should remain invisible. In the project, I propose the use of computer programs and specific publishing tools that should aid in rendering the translation and, thus, translator, more visible and allow even monolingual readers the opportunity to understand the complexities of another language and culture.

In the past four decades, linguistic and ethical issues associated with the translation of controversial texts have been discussed in the field of Translation Studies and Linguistics (e.g., Venuti, 1995/2008; Akbari, 2009; Tymoczko, 2012; Zulawnik, 2020). Researchers such as Venuti (1995/2008) and Tymoczko (2014) have placed particular focus on the power and visibility (or lack thereof) of the translator in the production of translations of controversial texts. Risks, whether they be political, cultural, or personal, associated with the translation of controversial texts, have not been discussed in great detail. This is in spite of prominent examples such as the mistranslation of political texts in the Middle-East and Europe (cf. e.g., Schäffner, 2004; Sharifian, 2009; El Shiekh, 2012), and the infamous case of Salman Rushdie's *The Satanic Verses*, which resulted in a *fatwa* that is linked to the assassination of the book's Japanese translator (Weisman, 1991) and to death threats followed by assassination attempts on three others (Fazzo, 1991; Yalman, 1994; Petrou, 2010).[1]

Issues related to the translation of political documents have been discussed more generally in Translation Studies (TS) literature by scholars such as Schäffner (1997, 2012), Tymoczko (e.g., 2000, 2014), Gentzler (Tymoczko & Gentzler, 2002), and Hermans (2009) but not so much in relation to translation methodology or what exactly ought to happen during the translation process. This gap in literature is particularly noticeable in Asian Studies: there is limited interest about the translation of controversial and/or political discourse in Asian Studies, let alone Japan-Korea relations. Translation of political materials, thus, must happen, although I would argue in a controlled environment. It is generally not a problem for a Japanese or Korean studies scholar, for instance, to translate from Japanese and Korean into English *excerpts* of controversial written works as part of research. The purpose of such an activity has academic value in its own right. And yet, it would be beneficial for someone who is not a speaker of Japanese/Korean (or other languages for that matter) also to have direct access to such cited works, as opposed to potentially biased interpretations, even if technically it would perhaps be impossible to call a translation a "perfect" copy of the source text because of the limitations of translation (e.g., translation of implicit meanings). Translation where the target text is deemed a "perfect" copy is, nevertheless, common practice particularly in political and government documents, where all translations are considered as authentic and true copies of the original (e.g., treaties of the European Union, United Nations, and Treaty on Basic Relations between Japan and the Republic of Korea). As proposed in this book, such full translations should be completed following a certain formula.

Translating a controversial text carries many of the same risks as the outright creation of a new (controversial) text. The nature of a text poses some risk to the translator as well as the readership. The translator may face backlash for having chosen to translate a text seen as 'inappropriate' or 'acidic', with potentially tangible implications on ability to travel freely as there is, for example, a law in South Korea which punishes authors of publications seen as either pro-Japanese or anti-Korean (Kr. *chin'il banminjok haengwi*, 친일반민족행위). Thus, the translator needs to be particularly sensitive to the environment in which the original text was published and to the range and nature of disputes that the original text engendered. It should be noted, however, that just because a source text is controversial, does not mean it should not be translated. One may argue that such is the case with, for example, the latest abridged German edition of *Mein Kampf* and *The Satanic Verses*.

Adolf Hitler's autobiography, *Mein Kampf* (1925), has long been regarded as a vile work, with publication and sale heavily restricted in some countries such as Austria and Germany. A number of translated editions have been made available over the years, some later sparking controversy due to translation choices and omission (e.g., Reynal & Hitchcock, 1939). In 2010, the *Institute of Contemporary History* (*Institut für Zeitgeschichte*) in Munich announced plans to publish a highly annotated edition of Hitler's work, titled *Hitler, Mein Kampf: Eine Kriitische Edition* (*Hitler, My Struggle: A Critical Edition*) to coincide with the expiry of the copyright so as "prevent neo-Nazi publications by putting out a commented, scholarly edition before that" (*New York Times*, 2010; *Spiegel Online*, 2010).

The issue surrounding the publication is of relevance to the project at hand, as the *Institute of Contemporary History*'s project may be seen as an example of an intra-linguistic translation with a pedagogical purpose. The idea to publish even a scholarly, heavily annotated edition of the work was met with mixed opinions, some organisations such as the *Zentrum für Antisemitismusforschung* (*Centre for Research on Antisemitism*) and *World Jewish Congress* as well as the Bavarian government which held the copyright, strongly objecting to republication in any form so as to respect victims of the Holocaust (*New York Times*, 2010; *BBC*, 2013/2016; *The Guardian*,

2016). Other organisations and scholars, however, welcomed the *Institute of Contemporary History*'s reasoning and justification for the project, considering the proposed publication a valuable historical resource (*New York Times*, 2010; *The Guardian*, 2015; *BBC*, 2016), whilst also noting that various editions of the work were already readily available online (*New York Times*, 2010), thus putting emphasis on the futility of trying to control readership. The new annotated edition of *Mein Kampf* was published in 2016 with orders for almost four times the initial print run and requests for translation into a number of languages (*The Guardian*, 2016).

Thus, a translator's choice of text may be questioned (or outright assumptions may be made), and, therefore, text choice requires justification. Translators may be accused of having political motivations themselves, if they select for translation a text which is widely seen as vilifying a certain group. Likewise, in the case of the project at hand, text selection and accompanying methodology are in the hands of the translator and, as discussed in later chapters, should be made with a clear pedagogical purpose in mind, as well as understanding of potential project risks including controversy such as that exemplified above. In the case of the text translated in this project, *Manga Kenkanryū* sold in excess of one million volumes under the publisher *Shinyusha Mook*, despite the ambivalence of the Japanese public's reception of the series at the time of its initial publication in 2005 (*New York Times*, 2005). As of 2011, the series has gone into reprint, suggesting ongoing popularity in some circles (Yamano, 2009).

It may be argued that Yamano's work both reflects and sustains the tense relationship between South Korea and Japan. Yamano credits *Manga Kenkanryū* as having played a key role in initiating the 'Hate *hallyu/kanryū*' movement Japan. The movement countered *hallyu/kanryū* (Kr. 한류, Jp. 韓流) or the 'Korean Wave', a period beginning around the year 2000 in which South Korean popular culture became highly fashionable, with South Korean soap operas, South Korean pop singers, and South Korean actors becoming increasingly visible in Japanese pop culture. Yamano claims the Korean Wave is simply 'hype' created by the mass media, as opposed to real valuable cultural exchange (Yamano, n.d.). Although Yamano's focus is on the recent prominence of Korean products in popular culture, he is often compared with the political *manga* author Kobayashi Yoshinori, who writes in controversial terms of the Japanese colonisation of Korea, between 1910–1945, of the second world war, and of the allied occupation of Japan (Liscutin, 2009, p. 190). Before publishing *Manga Kenkanryū*, Yamano was mainly active in the online publishing scene (Yamano, n.d.). Best known for the aforementioned comic, he is a self-proclaimed 'Korean Peninsula watcher' and claims to have "daringly travelled all over South Korea in order to find authentic materials" (Yamano, n.d.).[2]

To illustrate the potential risk stemming from debates about this *manga*, when approached by South Korean publishers interested in a Korean translation, a South Korean lawyer advised Yamano that South Korea's pro-Japanese/anti-Korean crimes law might result in his indictment if he were to visit South Korea (Yamano, 2005). Thus, the risks associated with the book and its translation may include the translator and author being denied entry into South Korea. If the author, translator, or publisher of a Korean translation were tried under a pro-Japanese/anti-Korean crimes law, the publicity might well also lead to verbal or even physical violence from right-wing activists in Korea and in Japan. Reportedly, both the author of *Manga Kenkanryū* and publishers of the Japanese translation of the comic written in reply, *Hyeomillyu* (*Hate Japanese Wave*), have received death threats from opposing organisations and individuals (2012).

Despite (or, perhaps, as a result of) its controversial nature, the comic managed to stay at the top of the book rankings on *Amazon.co.jp* for over a month (Liscutin, 2009, p. 173). Criticism of the comic has come from prominent figures in Japanese society such as Haku Shinkun – a Japanese politician of Korean descent (Yamano, 2006, p. 255) – and Japanese diplomat, Satō Masaru (*Nikkan Cyzo*, 2008). South Korean newspapers and media agencies such as *Chosun Ilbo, Hankook Ilbo, Dong'a Ilbo, Yonhap News Agency*, and *Seoul Broadcasting System* (*SBS*) were all quick to criticize the publication (*Chosun Ilbo*, 2011; Kim, 2011; Lee, 2011; Wang, 2009; Lee, 2012; Jeong, 2005). Some commentators have argued that these criticisms reveal anti-Japanese bias in the South Korean press: Nishimura (2006 – an author whose article features in Manga Kenkanryū) for example, writes that many South Korean media agencies made negative comments about the *manga* solely based on the provocative title and, at that, well before the comic was published (pp. 41–61).

There is risk associated with the translation of any discourse taking place in a politically heated context, as is also the case with non-translation. As to how broad this risk may be something that requires more attention, as although there has been some work on risk in translation by Akbari (2009), Tymoczko (2014), and Pym (2015), the scope has been largely limited to the risk of loss of earnings from an unpopular translation. I argue that there ought to be a distinction between such, what may be termed 'metaphorical' risk and 'tangible risk', which may pose real, physical danger to the translator and/or readership (Zulawnik, 2020).

Visibility and explication of the translation process of charged documents allows readers to gain insight into the nature and the subtleties of the political controversy. Insight such as this is beneficial, particularly when subtleties are at risk of being potentially overlooked due to focus on the issues themselves. Translators in a politically heated environment are in a situation where ultimately subject (what is being translated) tends to out-weigh method (how it was translated). Controversial documents such as the chosen text, *Manga Kenkanryū*, should be ideally translated with this scholarly, pedagogical purpose in mind. Doing so also acts as a method of risk management as the way in which a text is translated for such a purpose shall – or at least should– naturally differ from that translated for any other purpose. Translators who are also the commissioners of a translation must deal with discourse associated risks out of their own choice. In that sense, risk, tangible or not, is unavoidable and must be accepted. Thus, creating a methodology whereby the translation purpose is justified by being an aca-demic one, a text for scholarly purposes with full visibility of the translator, may be the only realistic method of risk management.

Notes

1 One of these assassination attempts resulted in the death of 37 bystanders, in an event known as the 'Sivas Massacre', where a mob of Islamic fundamental-ists stormed into a hotel where Aziz Nesin, the Turkish translator of *The Satanic Verses*, was attending a literary event, eventually burning down the premises (Yalman, 1994).

2 Since *Manga Kenkanryū*, Yamano has published four sequels with the same theme and is also the author of *Kenchūgokuryū* (Jp. 『嫌中国流』 – *Hate Chinese Wave*), published in 2008. More recently, Yamano turned to address domestic issues con-cerning ageism through the comic *Wakamono dorei jidai* (Jp. 『若者奴隷時代』 – *The age of the young slaves*, 2010) (Yamano, n.d). Yamano has also published a *manga* about the difficulties of becoming a *manga-ka* (*manga* artist) in Japan titled *Naruman*! (Jp. 『なる☆まん！』, 2010).

3 Japan and Korea (or 'Korea and Japan'?) – A Historical Background

The task of a translator undertaking a project such as this is to highlight issues stemming from language, whether it be word choice, tone, or stylistics. The political context of the selected source text (*Manga Kenkanryū*) is complex, and the multifaceted nature of Japan-South Korea relations requires explication, as does the spectrum of animosity coming from both sides.[1] This context directly affects the lexicon analysed in the translation and the careful choices made in translation. An understanding of anti-Japanese sentiment in South Korea is crucial to understand project-related risks, but it does not explicitly appear in the source text, whereas anti-Korean sentiment in Japan is evident simply by reading the source text and/or target text. The conflict is complex and two-sided, with translation choices having been made based on the understanding of the situation through readings and research in both languages. Therefore, the nature of South-Korean discourses about Japan also require attention here. The first section of the chapter pays attention to extreme political discourse from both sides of the Tsushima Strait and briefly traces the historical events that led not only to heated debate, including riots and growing jingoistic discourses on the part of populistic politicians.

Japan and Korea Pre-1945

Scholars have long recognised that Japan and Korea are both linguistically and, in many ways culturally, similar due to a common heritage. Just as these similarities and geographical proximity have allowed for interaction and the building of strong ties, so have the two nations' differences sparked widespread and ongoing conflict. Choe Nam-Seon (1890~1957), known as one of the 'three great geniuses' of the Joseon period, wrote an extensive history of Korea (Joseon) as part of his most famous work *Joseon Sangsik* (*Common knowledge about Joseon*).[2] In his work, Choe (1946/1997) carefully details the nature of Korea and Japan's close relationship using the

DOI: 10.4324/9781003167792-3

term *sunchi jiguk* (kr. 순치지국, 脣齒之國) or, literally, *countries [as close as the] lips and the teeth.*

South Korean scholarship on Korea-Japan relations, particularly in the 1980s and 1990s, such as that of the previous scholars, shows a trend towards a double-edged approach, construed under South-Korean nationalistic and cultural movements of the time; a mixture of seemingly objective commentary and adhesion to general government position (Park, 2000).[3] Thus, arguments about similarity or difference have always been intensely political, both in the colonial (1910–1945) and post-colonial periods.

In *Banil minjokjuwi reul neomeoseo* (*Getting over Anti-Japanese Nationalism*, my translation), Yu-ha Park (2000) notes that the aforementioned Korean scholars' move to emphasise similarities between Korean and Japanese culture with the aim of proving the former's 'superiority' is reminiscent of the strategy used by scholars of the Japanese Empire in preparation for (and during) the annexation of the Korean Peninsula during the late 19th and early 20th centuries. Park (2000) notes:

> What is interesting is the fact that such arguments are not exclusively Korean. The fact that Korea and Japan share similarities was strongly argued in the very same way during the Japanese occupation of Korea. This was the so-called *Japan-Joseon Common Ancestor Theory.*[4]
>
> (p. 50)

Park's (2000) analysis is accurate, as Duus (1995), for example, concurs that Japanese scholars recognised Korean influence on Japanese culture as well as the idea of a common Korean-Japanese ancestry from as early as the 19th century, before eventually utilising the concept as justification for the annexation of Korea, with Japan portrayed as an akin yet superior entity (also cf. Weiner, 1994). It should also be noted that various Japanese Meiji period scholars made similar arguments, including Kita Sadakichi (1871–1939), who argued "Joseon people must quickly assimilate as normal nationals [of the Japanese Empire] and become loyal subjects of His Majesty the Emperor [of Japan]. Not only because this will mean happiness for them, but also because it will manifest their forefather's customs" (1921).

Thus, as with other politically charged regions, there is not a single choice of lexicon that is not political in Japan-South Korea relations. The seemingly benign may also be rendered into something that is political in accordance with agendas of political factions currently in power all as a result of word choice and phrasing, be it intentional or not.

The most discussed conflict in Japan-Korea relations is, perhaps unsurprisingly, Japan's annexation of Korea in 1910. However, the roots of anti-Japanese sentiment in Korea and anti-Korean sentiment in Japan pre-date the 20th century in ways that also impact on the language used in the subject text. In particular, Japan's attempted invasions of Korea in 1274 and 1281 and again in 1592–1598 underpin many of these discourses. There has been abundant descriptive, rather than critical, literature in Korean (e.g. Choe, 2003; Kim, 2010, 2013), Japanese (e.g. Kamigaito, 2002/2004; Nakano, 2008; Kitajima, 2012), and English (e.g. Hulbert, 1905; Sansom, 1958; Turnbull, 2003; Swope, 2006/2015) about earlier historical conflicts between the predecessors of Japan and Korea's modern states.

Much of the focus, however, has been on the colonial period of 1910–1945, when Korea was annexed and subsequently part of the Japanese Empire. Issues pertaining to this period (and the preceding and following decades) such as the political lead up to Japan's annexation of Korea (Jp. *nikkan heigou*, 日韓併合), cultural assimilation (Jp. *kōminka seisaku*, 皇民化政策), atrocities, and post-war division of Korea have been widely dis-cussed by scholars from all areas of the spectrum with highly differentiated opinions, particularly in regard to the justification of said events (Mendl, 1995; Duus, 1995; Park, 2000; Ducke, 2002).

Debated issues include the justification and reasoning behind the Jap-anese annexation of Korea, language use once again playing a big role, with some far-right Japanese scholars and politicians, including the *Japa-nese Society of History Textbook Reform* (Jp. *Atarashii Rekishi Kyōkasho wo Tsukuru Kai*, 新しい歴史教科書をつくる会), arguing for the use of *advance* (Jp. *shinshutsu*, 進出) in place of *invasion* (Jp. *shinryaku*, 侵略), sparking outrage in much of Asia as well as international academic circles (Ducke, 2002).

Similarly, there has been much debate as to the terminology surrounding alleged forced prostitution in the Japanese military during the Pacific War. *Ianfu*, the term used most commonly in relation to this discourse, is written using the *kanji* compound *ian* (comfort) and *fu* (woman), but there have been moves by some groups to change this to the more charged *sex slaves* (Jp. *seidorei*, 性奴隷) on the grounds that using the euphemism created by the Japanese military system that employed or enslaved these women perpetuates the invisibility of the violence perpetrated against them. Word choice chosen to refer to these women by Japanese, Korean, and interna-tional scholars and organisations has been based on individual research and argumentation. Other examples include *prostitutes* (*baishunfu*, 売春婦) as well as *sex workers* (*seirōdōsha*, 性労働者; e.g., *United Nations*, 1996; *United Nations Commission on Human Rights*, 1998; Wada, 2011; Choe, 2014; Park, 2013/2014). The international nature of such debates adds to the complexity, as Japan and Korea in some ways utilise a shared lexicon in the form of Sino-Japanese and Sino-Korean words. The Japanese *baishunfu*, for example, although carrying the more general sense of *prostitute* in the Japanese and Korean languages (Kr. *maechunbu*, 매춘부, 売春婦), is sometimes translated in a more derogative way in Korea, using a term equivalent to *whore* (Kr. *changnyeo*, 창녀, 娼女).

After the Second World War, Korea was liberated only to plunge into the Korean War (1950–1953) after the 1948 division of the nation into the Republic of Korea (ROK) and Democratic People's Republic of Korea (DPRK). Whilst many scholars, particularly in South Korea (e.g., Kim, 2000; Kim et al., 2000), see the event as ultimately a result of Japanese imperialism, others argue that the events were inevitable due to earlier tensions between Soviet Russia and the United States (e.g., Hart-Landsberg, 1998; Seth, 2010; Oberdorfer & Carlin, 2013). Thus, there is not a single period that is not characterised by conflict and by conflict over the interpretation of events as well as associated terminology.

Japan and South Korea Post-1945

From the early 1960s till the 1980s, South Korea experienced rapid economic development commonly referred to as the *Miracle on the Han River* (Kr. *Hangangwi gijeok*, 한강의 기적, 漢江의 奇蹟), beginning after General Chung-Hee Park's coup *d'état* of 1961. The 1960s and 70s also witnessed greatly improved economic relations between South Korea and Japan following the South Korea-Japan Treaty on Basic Relations signed in 1965 (Kim, 1998, pp. 404–405). Although the treaty stipulated that all issues between Korea and Japan have been settled (and nullified the Ganghwa Treaty of 1910), there has been heated debated in recent history as to whether or not it accounted for Japan's war crimes and compensation. The current official Japanese stance is that compensation was completed in the 1960s as part of a loan and compensations made to the South Korean government, with further supplementation as part of the 2016 agreement for Japan to pay one billion yen to a fund supporting surviving victims.

1982 saw the beginning of increased tensions between Japan and South Korea, particularly in relation to the 'Japanese History Textbook problem,' which has also continued through to this day. The South Korean and Chinese governments argue that Japanese history textbooks, particularly ones proposed by the Japanese Society for History Book Reform (the latter of which have been adopted by a very small number of Japanese schools after government approval in 2001) try to beautify Japan's military past, including, as aforementioned, that of the comfort women, the annexation of the Korean Peninsula in 1910, as well as illustrating the Asia Pacific War as a defensive war.

Based on previously discussed poll results (East Asia Institute, 2013, 2014, 2015, 2016, 2017), as well as recent *BBC* polls (2011, 2012, 2013), anti-Japanese sentiment in South Korea may be seen as widespread, manifesting in popular channels such as literature (discussed later) and television, education, and politics (Cheong, 1991; Lee & Moon, 2002). Ironically, however, the South Korean government is often criticised by South Korean netizens as being in fact 'pro-Japanese'. Seog-Yeong Choi (2010) in *Kimchi Aegukjuwi* (*Kimchi Patriotism*, my translation) argues that anti-Japanese sentiment in South Korea is an 'alibi' for perceived pro-Japanese behaviour (the 'crime'), writing that anti-Japanese sentiment felt by South Koreans is much stronger than that of ethnic Korean ('Zainichi') residents in Japan, as the former is a product of government, media, and academia profiteering as anti-Japanese sentiment is "the easiest thing to feed the people" (pp. 246–258). Choi (2010) also notes that such "meaningless anti-Japanese sentiment", often manifested by even the youngest of South Koreans, is worse than that seen in the population directly affected by Japanese colonialism (pp. 246–247). In *South Korea's Diplomacy Policies* (Kim et al., 1998) Kim Jae-Ho summarises his chapter on South Korea-Japan relations noting that whereas early generations – or the 'Japanese language generation' – had mixed feelings about Japan due to having directly experienced the colonial period, the 'hangeul generation' that followed and is currently in control of South Korean society, "developed through strong anti-Japanese education and developed with almost no knowledge or information about Japan" (pp. 413–414).

As shall be discussed in the following section, 20 years since this statement, very little has changed. After a short period of improved relations from around 1999~2010, affairs have reached new lows, with a very bleak outlook. An example is Kim Jin-Myeong's anti-Japanese best-seller novel *Mugunghwa Ggochi Pieosseumnida* (*A Rose of Sharon has Bloomed*, my translation), a book that illustrates a phantasy whereby a unified Korea strikes Japan with nuclear weapons. Park (2000) writes of Kim's book:

> [when A Rose of Sharon has Bloomed first came out in the early 90s] the Korean public's excitement (as opposed to criticism) at Kim's work proved that this [violent/militaristic] unconscious was not exclusive to the author, but a thing of the majority. In this sense, the A Rose of Sharon has Bloomed phenomenon was an 'event' that frankly revealed South Korea's late 20th century unconscious. That is because everyone agreed to unconscious affirmation of violence whereby a country, rather than criticising another's physical 'violence', can inflict the same type of 'violence' whenever there is a chance and enough strength to do so.
>
> (p. 73)

Similar publications, although perhaps not as popular, can also be seen in Japan. *Manga Kenkanryū* (2005) falls into the very same category as these novels and, as mentioned in the first chapter, enjoyed considerable popularity having now sold over one million copies (Yamano, 2010). Other Japanese works that created controversy both in Japan and South Korea include Park Tae-Hyeok's critical essay about South Korea *Minikui Kankokujin* (Jp. 醜い韓国人) (*Ugly South Koreans*, 1993, my translation). Although proving a bestseller in Japan, this book created heated debate at a time when Japan-South Korea relations were already frail due to political issues surrounding history textbooks, the 'comfort women', and the territorial dispute surrounding Liancourt Rocks. There was widespread debate in Japan and South Korea (upon release of a translation) as to whether the book was really written by a Korean, or by Kase Hideaki, a Japanese critic (Hwang & Shin, 1993). Kase (1995), who wrote an afterword to the work, later denied this to be his work in a book he claims he wrote with the 'original' Korean author, Tae-Hyuk Park, titled *Ugly South Koreans –Historical Verification Edition* (Jp. 醜い韓国人 - 歴史検証編). The book sparked a number of South Korean spin-offs, including Yeong-Chun Lim's *An ugly South Korean answers to Japan* (1994) and *Ugly South Koreans or Ugly Japanese?* (1996).

In the midst of such animosity, towards the turn of the 21st century, there were some signs of bi-lateral relations improving, at least on a non-political level, something that has been sometimes accredited to the manifestation of the *Hallyu* (Korean Wave) phenomenon to Japan. The Korean Wave – or 'South Korean Cultural Wave' (Kim, 2012) – is said to have first appeared in Asia towards 2000 (Shin et al., 2006, pp. 14–19; Ogura, 2005, pp. 52–53). Making its mark in Japan in 2002, the Korean Wave was triggered by widespread fanfare for the television soap opera *Winter Sonata* (*Digital Daijisen*, 2012). Japanese interest in South Korea increased in the wake of this series, with the introduction of numerous other soap operas (Ogura, 2005, p. 9). The year 2002 saw the co-hosting of the Japan-Korea FIFA World Cup, which, coupled with the introduction of South Korean popular music ('K-Pop') to the Japanese music market, secured South Korea's image as a 'trendy' destination amongst many Japanese (Ogura, 2005, pp. 9–10).

This very sudden jump in awareness about South Korean popular culture also eventually provoked increased anti-Korean sentiment and criticism from 'uninterested' Japanese or, as Sakamoto (2011) terms it, a nationalistic online following "confined within niche online communities, hardly representative of civil society". Sakamoto and Allen (2007) contextualise the origins of such sentiment (eventually illustrated in 2005 through the publication *Manga Kenkanryū*) as the "discursive dominance of moderate conservatism" in post-1990 Japan being superimposed by discourses of nationalism and revisionism sometimes labelled by its proponents as liberal history, with *Manga Kenkanryū* appearing as part of this shift. Since the end of 2012, there has been increasing tension due to South Korea's former president Myung-Bak Lee's visit to the Dokdo/Takeshima Islets, followed by remarks about Japan's Emperor, as well as more visible nationalism from the Liberal Democratic Party of Japan (*Jimintō*) and security issues relating to North Korea.

The translation of *Manga Kenkanryū* thus required appreciation and understanding of the aforementioned issues concerning history and politics in the sphere of Japan-South Korea relations, as most contribute to form the subject matter of the volume, thus also constituting the translation method-ology. Namely, the translation required careful consideration of the project purpose, word choice, and additional translator input based on the broader context of academic discussion.

Notes

1 In this chapter, Korea refers to unified Korea prior to 1945 and the Republic of Korea (i.e., South Korea) post 1945.
2 *Joseon samdae cheonjae* (Kr. 조선 3대 천재, 朝鮮三大天才, my translation).
3 One such work by a South Korean scholar includes *Original Form of the Korean/Japanese Peoples –a different flower blooms from the same seed* (Kr. 한-일 민족의 원형: 같은 씨에서 다른꽃이 핀다, 韓-日 民族의 原型: 같은 씨에서 다른꽃이 핀다) by Yong-Un Kim (1989) (my translation).
4 My translation. *Japan-Joseon Common Ancestor Theory* is known as *Nissen Dousou ron* (日鮮同祖論) in Japanese, and *Ilseon Dongjo ron* (일선동조론, 日鮮同祖論) in Korean. For criticism of Sadakichi see for example Oguma, 1995.

4   Translation, Culture, and Functionalism

When translating a text such as that selected as part of this project it would seem crucial to consider culture: there is now widespread recognition that translation is much more than simple word transfer, largely as a result of the "cultural turn" in Translation Studies, a paradigm shift that was gradually brought about by interdisciplinary research conducted from around the 1980s, or 1960s/1970s if considering relevant findings by 'the Russian formalists' and members of the so called 'invisible college' (notably including Evan-Zohar, Toury, and Holmes) (Hermans, 1999). Research pertaining to the cultural turn significantly altered the way in which translation theorists perceive the act of translating and its nature as a multifaceted discourse. One of the results has been a gradual shift of focus from often atomic ST based analysis, to that of the TT, and more importantly, the target context(s).

Use of the term 'turn' has been criticised by some scholars such as Anthony Pym (2011), a stance reflective of his generally strict stance towards many of the generalisations prominent in TS including *skopos*, which he argues should be replaced with simple terms (in this case, simply 'purpose'). Indeed, there has been much debate in recent years as to the use of translation theory in the 'real world' in aspects such as translator ethics and relevance of translation theories (e.g., Chesterman & Wagner, 2002), a valid point of discussion as very few professional translators consciously apply translation theory to their projects.

The cultural turn's significance is made explicit by Theo Hermans (1999, pp. 9–16) as having helped overhaul TT and target context-based research. This overhaul was achieved through the application of previously overlooked theories and research from other fields such as philosophy by scholars such as Venuti (e.g., 1992, 2003), Scott (2012), and Norris (2002), with particular focus on Derrida and deconstruction. A significant step towards the cultural turn is found in research that was conducted from the early 1970s by the 'Functionalists', notably including scholars such as Reiß, Vermeer, Nord, and Holz-Mänttäri (cf. Reiß, 1971/2000; Nord, 1988/2005; Vermeer, 1989/2004; Holz-Mänttäri, 1984/1986). As their name may suggest,

DOI: 10.4324/9781003167792-4

the Functionalists focused on aspects concerning the function of texts in translation with particular attention to the TT, in what may be seen as a sub-set of more general action theory (Baker & Malmkjær, 2001, pp. 3–5).

Within these early theories, *skopostheorie* has been most prominently discussed by TS scholars since its detailed introduction in 1984 in Vermeer and Reiß' *Grundlegung einer allgemeine Translationstheorie* (*Groundwork for a General Theory of Translation*). One of the issues most commonly raised during analysis of *skopostheorie* is the fact that it grants the translator considerable freedom as to how to translate. What is in need of particular attention as part of the project at hand is that such freedom is granted in the style of *finis coronat opus*. In other words, as long as the purpose (*skopos*) of the TT is met, practically any method deemed adequate by the commissioner (client) can be applied during the translation process (Hatim, 2001, pp. 74–75; Nord, 2001, p. 29; Chesterman & Wagner, 2002, pp. 40–43; Munday, 2012, pp. 122–126). The theory, however, is not as 'bare-bones' as may seem at first glance. Notably, the translator's approach must be justified (*begründen*) as appropriate for the *skopos/skopoi* in question (Nord, 2001, pp. 28–29; Hatim, 2001, pp. 74–75).

Christiane Nord, who similarly advocates a Functional Linguistics approach to translation, has at times criticised the way in which *skopostheorie* is described by Vermeer (1984), as he does not stress the importance of 'loyalty', thus giving the impression that 'anything goes' (Munday, 2012, p. 123; Nord, 2001, pp. 110–130). Nord (2001) however clarifies the issue through a definition of 'loyalty':

> [Loyalty is] this responsibility translators have towards their partners in translational interaction. Loyalty commits the translator bilaterally to the source and the target sides. It must not be mixed up with fidelity and faithfulness, concepts that usually refer to a relationship holding between the source and target texts. Loyalty is an interpersonal category referring to a social relationship between people.
>
> (p. 125)

In case of the project at hand, which is self-commissioned, loyalty may be seen as being between the translator and anticipated readership to which the project purpose is created to cater. Hatim (2009) argues that, although the simple answer to the question of *who actually decides the skopos?* is the 'client', translation briefs may be insufficiently detailed from a methodological point of view (p. 40). In order to try and clarify this issue, Hatim (2009) states that:

> To deal with [the issue of briefs lacking detail in regard to translation methodology] *skopos* theory entertains the general assumption that

there will generally be a 'standard' way (sanctioned by the professional community of translators, for example) of proceeding to accomplish a particular translation task. . . . [And] there is also the case where no 'client' is particularly envisaged and where no purpose is specified.

The issue of commission directly relates to the much broader discourse of 'patronage', discussed in great detail by scholars such as Lefevere (e.g., 1985/1992), Chesterman (e.g., 1997), Hatim (e.g., 2001), and Munday (2001). Although there is a lack of consensus as to what exact role(s) patronage plays in the act of translation, patronage may be defined as influence or power stemming from either individuals or institutions, which can, depending on circumstances, either help or hinder the progression of the translation task (Lefevere, 1992). In a project funded by a government institution, for example, the institution may be seen as effectively playing the role of a commissioner, exerting influence on the translation process through economic and/or other means.

'Patronage' may, therefore, be seen as an external force when compared to 'loyalty' discussed earlier in this chapter. The focus of this book, however, is on a project where the translator has self-commissioned the translation as part of a pedagogical activity. There may, of course, always be external forces not unlike those pertaining to the discourse of patronage (e.g., research funding); however, the approach presented here is one where both the translator and translation are highly visible and open to reader scrutiny. Although beyond the scope of this project, it should also be noted that a further dimension to the (dis)placement and decision making of a translator within the discourse of patronage may also be seen through Gideon Toury's idea of 'translation norms' and, in particular, 'initial' and then 'preliminary norms' (Toury, 1978/2012).

Gideon Toury (1995/2012), a co-creator of Descriptive Translation Studies (DTS), a sub-field of Translation Studies specifically focusing on translation analysis, proposes a number of 'norms' and rules' that may be used to identify and distinguish actions taken by translators before and/or during the translation process. 'Initial norms' refer to a choice made by the translator(s) to either follow norms found within the ST or TT culture and language, making the end product either 'adequate' or 'acceptable', respectively (Toury, 1995/2012). Adequate and acceptable translation, although not mutually exclusive, are useful in determining the translator's general approach to translation, with adequate translations being more common in didactic tasks such as that at hand (i.e., ST focus). The translator's norm-determined decision making within this discourse directly relates back to the issue of patronage discussed earlier in this chapter, as patronage often governs these decisions. The autonomist nature of the translator as a commissioner in this particular task therefore allows for a clearer approach, which, in theory, should be easy to identify as having produced a ST-oriented, 'adequate' translation as per the initial norms.

Although the main purpose of translating *Manga Kenkanryū* (i.e. creation of a scholarly resource) is the overriding factor in all translation decisions made as part of this project, much like in *skopostheorie*, it is no more than a general 'aim'. A literal translation approach, for example, would be an ideal choice in the translation of controversial, politically charged materials; the ST message is largely preserved 'as is'. Such an approach, however, may not achieve the project purpose if the readers, that is, a general academic audience, have trouble comprehending certain culturally bound meanings, slang, or difficult historical terms.

In light of the project circumstances, *skopostheorie* poses a number of serious questions. The concept of 'purpose' and its overriding effect on translatorial action (shift of focus from ST to TT) is useful, but whether or not this is enough to constitute a theoretical framework leaves room for doubt. Subsequently, whilst acknowledging the importance of what *skopostheorie* has done for TS, a choice should be made to apply only that which is most useful, namely, the pragmatic concept of a TT determined by purpose. Movement towards supplementing *skopostheorie* (i.e. no commissioner and lack of translation methodology) may be initiated through analysis of Nord's (2001) 'purposeful translation' approach, another key functionalist theory.

Christiane Nord's (2001) purposeful translation approach offers a considerably more detailed functionalist model compared to that of Vermeer's *skopostheorie*, drawing upon House (1977) and Reiß' (1977) works on text types (p. 47). First mentioned in *Text Analysis in Translation* (1988), Nord's (2005) approach begins with the definition of two basic modes of text transfer, namely 'documentary' and 'instrumental' translation (pp. 80–84). Documentary and instrumental translation may be summarised as follows: documentary translation, as its name may suggest, serves as a method of 'documenting' ST information (Nord, 2005, p. 72), whereby the ST is "simply reproduced, with no special allowances made for the target context" (Hatim, 2001, p. 89). A TT achieved following the documentary translation method allows the reader full access to concepts in the ST through techniques such as literal translation and 'exoticisation' (Hatim, 2001, p. 89), albeit never posing itself as a fluent (Munday, 2012, p. 126) or idiomatic translation (cf. Larson, 1998, pp. 18–20). 'Exoticisation' is defined by Nord (2005) as a method that preserves local flavour of the ST (p. 81). Munday (2012) lists examples such as the German words 'Quark', 'Roggenbrot' and 'Wurst' remaining in German in the TT (p. 126). See section on 'foreignisation' (i.e. 3.3.1).

Instrumental translation is aimed at the production of an *instrument* for a new communicative interaction between the source-culture and a target-culture audience in the target language (Nord, 2001, p. 47), signifying that the TT is read as a work originally written in the target language (Munday, 2012, p. 126). Of the two modes, it is quite clear that documentary translation is the right option for the project at hand, as the purpose is a pedagogical one. Before it is deemed part of the methodology, however, it is important to review the criteria. In order to review documentary translation's relevance to the translation of *Hate Hallyu: The Comic* it would be best to refer to a table summarising the modes different criteria:

Table 4.1 Documentary translation (Nord, 2001, p. 48)

Function of translation	Document of source-culture communicative interaction for target-culture readership			
Function of target text	Metatextual function			
Type of translation	**DOCUMENTARY TRANSLATION**			
Form of translation	Interlineal translation	Literal translation	Philological translation	Exoticising translation
Purpose of translation	Reproduction of SL system	Reproduction of SL form	Reproduction of ST form + content	Reproduction of ST form, content + situation
Focus of translation process	Structures of SL lexis + syntax	Lexical units of ST	Syntactical units of ST	Textual units of ST
Example	Comparative linguistics	Quotations in news text	Greek and Latin Classics	Modern literary prose

The main purpose of the project qualifies well for a documentary translation mode, as per Table 4.1. The translation clearly has a 'metatextual' function, namely, to document a source-culture communicative interaction for a target culture readership. The translation of *Hate Hallyu: The Comic* for scholarly purposes should be between that of a literal and philological one, providing literal renditions of the ST accompanied by carefully structured translator's notes where necessary. In order to maintain fidelity, the focus of the translation approach is on structures and lexical, syntactical, and textual units of the ST rather than aesthetic factors.

As Nord's two modes of translation practically embody all types of translation (it is hard to imagine a translation that is neither documentary nor instrumental), it is quite obvious that the translation of *Hate Hallyu: The*

Comic (with its new purpose) too finds a place. Had the purpose been, for example, for the TT to have a similar effect on target readers as the ST had on those from the source culture, instrumental translation would have been a more appropriate choice. Having said that, the 'documentary translation' mode does provide a good general approach for the translation of *Hate Hallyu: The Comic*.

Multi-modal Translation

Here, it is necessary to discuss the comic book medium which *Manga Kenkanryū* is part of. Comic translation in general, be it that of graphic novels, Western comics or *manga*, is seen as having been limited in spite of a broad readership and a history intertwined with translating (Zanettin, 2008, p. 19). Starting with Kaindl (1999), there is now, nevertheless, steadily growing scholarship, particularly with focus on *manga* translation (e.g., O'Hagan, 2006), including my own preliminary research (2016), which focused on the partial comparative translation of *Hate Hallyu: The Comic* and *Hate Japanese Wave* (the South Korean comic written in reply to the former). Of further relevance is research from related fields that discuss multi-modal materials such as, for example, audio-visual translation and the task of subtitling and fansubbing (e.g., Cintas, 2012; Massidda, 2015; Pedersen, 2018), detailed discussion of which is beyond the scope of this project but would make an interesting comparative study.

The work containing this chapter, titled *Manga Vision* (Pasfield-Neofitou & Sell, 2016), discusses issues such as the translation of onomatopoeia and mimesis (Sell & Pasfield-Nofitou, 2016) as well more general issues concerning the medium such as communication and engagement (e.g., Robertson, 2016; Lee & Armour, 2016) and impact of the medium on culture (e.g., Baudinette, 2016; Bell, 2016). Especially relevant to this project is the scholarship contained in *Comics in Translation* (2008), where the comic format sees discussion relating to translation methodology. Particular attention is paid to what could be generally summarised as constituent of the 'foreignisation' versus 'domestication' debate, terms coined by Lawrence Venuti, based on a distinction made by Schleiermacher in the early 19th century (Rota, 2008, p. 84). It is important to consider foreignisation with reference to *manga* translation as this can provide a clearer, more focused definition ahead of the concept's application. Foreignisation is a concept of particular significance to this project widely associated with ethics as well as the *manga* medium. In accordance with the project purpose (the TT function) and documentary translation approach defined in section 2.3, the translation should be, to some extent, literal so as to preserve culturally and linguistically important elements of the ST. Venuti (1995/2008) defines foreignisation as 'a process that allows the original work to resist integration and to maintain its features' in contrast to domestication, which is 'an ethnocentric reduction of the foreign text to target language cultural values' (p. 20). The consensus regarding foreignisation amongst the scholars addressing Japanese *manga* translation into other languages in *Comics in Translation* is that it has become a predominant translation norm (Rota, 2008, p. 85; Jüngst, 2008a, p. 74; Zanettin, 2008, p. 22).[1] In the case of this project, a foreignising approach is justified by the purpose as discussed in the first chapter; however, when considering the fact that foreignisation is a norm in *manga* translation, the approach gains increased importance, as the medium places translatorial limitations (such as editing of visual elements) on the project.

The reasons behind a foreignising approach in comic translation are plentiful. For example, *manga* readership often harbours expectations for there to be a certain 'Japaneseness' or 'Japonismé' when reading translated works (Zanettin, 2008a, p. 24; Jüngst, 2008a, pp. 68, 74). Such perceived 'Japaneseness' as a tool in globalising Japanese culture has been discussed by O'Hagan (2006), not just in the domain of manga but also anime and video games. Literal translation of any kind, to a certain extent, can be seen as foreignisation; according to Jüngst (2008a), there has been a gradual shift from 'dynamic' to more 'formal' equivalence in *manga* translation through the employment of foreignisation, seen in regard to visual elements, onomatopoeias, and the verbal text (pp. 50–51).[2] The terms 'formal' and 'dynamic' equivalence were first coined by Bible translator Eugene Nida (Hatim, 2001, p. 18) in the 1960s to replace 'obsolete' terms such as 'literal', 'free', and 'faithful' translation (Munday, 2012, p. 66). As defined by Nida (1964) the former "focuses attention on the message itself, in both form and content" whilst with the latter "the relationship between receptor and message should be substantially the same as that which existed between the original receptors and the message" (p. 159) and are therefore to a large extent akin to Nord's 'documentary' and 'instrumental' modes of translation. A caveat to note here, however, is that domestication and foreignisation are not part of a mutually exclusive dichotomy. There has been, for example, criticism of highly foreignising approaches 'exotifying' the source text, making it deliberately stand out to cater to readership liking (Bassnett & Lefevere, 1990). Exoticisation is an important point to note, particularly in regard to *manga* translation. As aforementioned, there have been shifts in the general approach taken in translating *manga* in the 1980s, seeing a general trend towards domestication that included the editing of onomatopoeia and flipping of images so as to accommodate the left-right reading direction of most non-Japanese readerships.

Although the readership defined by the main project *skopos* in this case is certainly not a *manga* fan-base, *manga* is the medium of the ST. The medium

should therefore be preserved, as a change to book format would eliminate visual features, which is unacceptable. Hence, a level of foreignisation
above that of a standard *manga* translation should be expected, although
not to the extent that the ST is somehow made unduly 'exotic'. Increased
foreignisation calls for a preface and translator's notes so as to increase
comprehension and intra-textual cohesion; the use of notes as an aid is quite
common in *manga* translation (Jüngst, 2008a, pp. 50–74). Jüngst (2008a)
mentions use of footnotes in *manga* of both an educational (instructive) and
leisurely (supplementary) kind. According to Jüngst (2008a), footnotes are
often used in *manga*, which retain Japanese historical terms and cultural
items (pp. 56–57).

Strictly speaking, foreignisation in terms of *manga* translation spans from
retaining the reading direction of the ST (Cheetham, 2010, pp. 45–46), to
keeping onomatopoeias in the SL form (Jüngst, 2008a, pp. 64–67). However, considering Hatim's (2001) emphasis that foreignisation and domestication are not binary concepts, not all foreignising methods have to be
applied. In this project, for example, although the ST reading order has been
preserved, in the case of onomatopoeias a choice has been made to apply
a domesticating approach and translate. Pym (1996) asks whether scholars
should be at all surprised there is a trend towards 'fluency' in a culture as
influential as that of the Anglophone world (p. 171). I would argue that
such a statement is beyond the point Venuti (1995/2008) is trying to make.
Although scholars should not be surprised by a trend towards fluency based
upon Pym's (1996) argument, Venuti's (1995/2008) work, rather than showing 'surprise', is trying to do something more significant: it is changing
Anglo-centric society so that it is more receiving of other cultures. In the
case of this project, I am trying to introduce sources and subtleties in English otherwise potentially overlooked in the context of Japan-South Korea
relations.

Munday (2012) concedes that a foreignising approach indeed does
allow the receiving culture to be more aware of the foreign origins of the
translation. That is, the reader is not led to believe that the text that is being
read is an original, through the highlighting of 'foreign identity' (p. 219).
Hatim (2001) also concurs, emphasising the risks of a domesticating
approach as having an exclusionary impact on the source culture values,
forming perceptions and stereotypes of national identities (p. 46). Nevertheless, as with all other dichotomies and as discussed earlier, domestication and foreignisation should not be treated as binary opposites but part
of a continuum (cf. Table 4.2), which relates to "ethical choices made by
the translator in order to expand the receiving culture's range" (Munday,
2012, p. 220).

Table 4.2 Domestication and foreignisation: ethical and discursive levels (Munday, 2012, p. 221)

Ethical Level	Domestication ←————————————→	Foreignisation
	(Conforming to TL culture values)	(making visible the foreign)
Discursive Level	Fluency ←————————————→	Resistancy
	('Transparent reading', assimilated to TL norms)	(Resistant reading, challenging TL norms)

Once again, ironically, in the case of the source medium (*manga*), there is more of a trend to foreignise (and thus also sometimes exoticise) translations, as that is something sought after by readers who are often also interested in Japanese culture. In my project, although I employ foreignising techniques, I do so arguing for the need for the translation of a wide range of texts from a pedagogical perspective, certainly not so as to 'exoticise' the source text. Nevertheless, the consideration of the *manga* comic medium in relation to the project *skopos* and mode of translation (documentary translation) has allowed for the ascertainment of a more concrete translation approach, that is, what could perhaps be termed as 'supplemented foreignisation'.

Translation and Risk

The importance of approach is further accentuated when the issue of risk in translation is brought forth. Risk is a key issue discussed in the project at hand, with some of its facets illustrated in the earlier discussion about Japan-Korea relations. No matter how noble the project purpose, there is always bound to be some kind of risk associated, be it economic or of a more serious nature, and, as noted by my wise grandfather Adam in the introduction, we may simply have to find some white linen to wrap ourselves in.

Although very limited compared to the plethora of scholarship discussing other issues in TS, scholars such as Akbari (2009) and Pym (2010) have made contributions to 'Risk Management in Translation'. As mentioned earlier, much of the work, however, has addressed 'economic' risk associated with commercial success/failure. The project-associated risk, as is the case in this project, can also potentially be of a physically dangerous nature, affecting not only the translator but, more importantly, the client (commissioner) and readership. Inadequately managed risk of any kind can lead to any number of negative outcomes, as outlined by Akbari (2009) in *Risk Management in Translation*.[3] Akbari (2009) thoroughly analyses different kinds of project risk, dividing them into five translation activities:

'Market', 'Financial', 'Project', 'Production Process', and 'Product' risks (pp. 1–2). In the case of this project, however, only 'Production Process' and 'Product 'risks are of relevance, as the *skopos* is not subject to 'commercial' issues. 'Production Process' and 'Product' risks are of significance, as they relate to the act of translation (possible mistranslations), and 'acceptability' (readership reception), respectively (Akbari, 2009, pp. 2–5). The relevance of translation risk management is reinforced by Pym (2010), who asserts that translators must carefully judge which risks pose the most danger. Pym (2010) places risk into a spectrum ranging from 'very low' to 'very high' risk (pp. 1–4) and even briefly alludes to 'real', 'dangerous' risk.[4] As discussed in the introduction, examples of such risk in translation are numerous, ranging from the mistranslation of political texts (Schäffner, 2004; Sharifian, 2009; El Shiekh, 2012) to fallout following translation of literature such as the *Satanic Verses* (Weisman, 1991).

Although in the case of this project, most likely 'low-risk', the scale of such *potentially* dangerous factors should not be overlooked. Here, it must also be noted that such seemingly 'metaphorical' risk (e.g., misunderstanding of the TT by readers), too, can bring 'real', 'physical' outcomes upon the translator (Maier, 2007, p. 11), and other parties, including the commissioner and readership.[5] In terms of the task at hand, this may include, as discussed earlier, potential bans from entering South Korea or prosecution based on perceived defamation. The main type of risk requiring careful consideration, however, is that of a (con)textual nature, in other words, translator bias and (un)intentionally misleading readers.

The method of what Akbari (2009) terms 'Risk Treatment' is categorised as 'Risk Avoidance', 'Risk Reduction'/'Mitigation', 'Risk Transfer', and 'Risk Retention' (p. 5). Examples of such methods may include: choosing not to engage in a translation after consideration of the risks (avoidance); inclusion of a translator's forward/notes so as to disambiguate precarious terms and explain the translator's approach and/or word-for-word translation or transliteration so as to retain important lexical features found in the ST (thus increasing fidelity to the ST; reduction/mitigation); conducting a group translation (risk transfer); and finally, decision to accept risk (retention) (Akbari, 2009, pp. 1–5). As asserted earlier, the gravest risk requiring consideration in the project at hand, is the 'misleading of the readership' through inaccurate translations (production process and product risks). Following an ethical model of risk retention and reduction, in all its imperfection, combined with a foreignising approach, would seem to be the safest path. Indeed, as exemplified in the introduction and brief historical background of Japan-Korea relations, the translation of political texts or texts that are intertwined with political discourse or any kind of ideology can pose ethical challenges for the translator (Àlvarez & Vidal, 1993; Baker,

2006; Pérez, 2014). Furthermore, work in the domain of multi-modal and audio-visual translation poses text-type specific issues relating to power and ideology (O'Hagan, 2006; Cintas, 2012; Katan, 2018).

The translation of controversial material, the origin of 'controversy' and the risks the act of translating controversial material poses, may be seen through many lenses and, thus, discussed in relation to a number of broad discourses such as, for example, 'power'. Baker (2006) writes on power's influence on conflict:

> Definitions of conflict inevitably draw on notions of power, and vice versa. Traditional scholarship assumed that power is something that some people have over others. Some theorists of power, such as Bachrach and Baratz (1962, 1970), further insisted that power is only present in situations of observable conflict, where one party forces another to act against its will or what it perceives to be its own interest. More robust definitions of power, however, acknowledge that the supreme exercise of power involves shaping and influencing another party's desires and wants in such a way as to avert observable conflict, that 'the most effective and insidious use of power is to prevent . . . conflict from arising in the first place'.
>
> (Lukes, 1974, p. 23)

Bassnett (1996) further notes that "the study and practice of translation is inevitably an exploration of power relationships within textual practice that reflect power structures within the wider cultural context". Baker (2006) and Bassnett's (1996) discussion and definitions of power related directly to the cultural turn in translation and may be further expanded through understanding of the discourse of 'patronage' discussed earlier.

The influence of power is something that a translator has to be well-aware of when making a choice to translate based on, for example, 'preliminary norms' (Toury, 2012), as this will decide the success of the project (or accomplishment of *skopos*). This is of course mostly the case when the project is self-commissioned. In situations where the translator has little choice as to whether to translate or not (or what approach to take), the power relationship is much more complex (Àlvarez & Vidal, 1996). I argue, on a number of occasions, that translating for a clearly pedagogical purpose whilst employing techniques such as extended translator's notes most often associated with such an approach (cf., e.g., Katan, 2018) may be a good way of mitigating various project related risks whilst allowing for better informed discussions in relation to complex issues with the involvement of a broader range of the public (the target readership).

A widely discussed view (e.g. Buden, 2006; Bellos, 2012) is that translation is 'impossible', especially when considering concepts such as semantic equivalence. But, perhaps even more intriguing than this is translatability with reference to ideology, as translating political texts when viewed from an ethical or philosophical perspective, as discussed in this chapter, goes beyond a matter of replacing words or even meanings. A TT may be received in any number of ways, not only by the target audience/culture but also that of the source culture/language through the media, as exemplified by the case of the translations of Salman Rushdie's novel the *Satanic Verses*.

Reception, thus, depends on any number of factors including – but not limited to – the source text (and almost anything to do with it, as shall be discussed in the following chapter), translation method, text-type, sending/receiving culture (or *habitus*), parties involved (influences such as that discussed as part of the discourse of patronage), and so on. Attaining a clear *skopos* or simply *purpose* is only the first step. There is need to pose the following question: how can something as subjective as 'success' in translation be achieved or even determined when there are so many factors, so many 'unknowns' (e.g., potential risks, ethical pitfalls) involved?

Notes

1 This is not always necessarily the case with comics other than *manga* (i.e. Western style comics) and is something that is discussed in detail in *Comics in Translation* (Jüngst, 2008a, 2008b; Zitawi, 2008; Rota, 2008; Zanettin, 2008b).

2 One such good example is that of Tokyopop's '100% authentic manga' format (CBR, 2003).

3 Emily Apter (2006) in *The Translation Zone: A New Comparative Literature*, alludes to the notion that translation may very well be regarded as a 'weapon of war' (p. 16).

4 Pym (2010) asserts "If and when [translators] misjudge the risks and give real offence, real damage can result", adding "Those of us who train translators should be thinking in terms of those kinds of actual conflict, where the risks are something more than *metaphorical* [emphasis added]" (p. 10).

5 Maier (2007), upon discussing some of the hardships of interpreters at Guantanamo, states: "The interesting thing for a discussion of translation, though, is the suggestion that translating or interpreting can cause such disease that one's organism becomes literally (as opposed to metaphorically) diseased." (p. 11)

5 Translating Controversy and 'Contraverse' – A Methodology

We are all mediators, translators.

– Jacques Derrida

The primary aim of my research was to develop and evaluate a new methodology for the successful translation of controversial texts such as *Manga Kenkanryū*. I argue that this may be achieved through the formulation of a pedagogical project purpose with recognition of translator power and associated responsibility as well as commitment to guiding the readership through the use of new technology that allows for increased visibility of the translator, something I term the 'Compass of Translation'. The definition of 'success' requires clarification: the translation's commissioner and their view of 'success' may not necessarily be the same as that of the translator, the information conduit or commissioner, not only in the sense of a traditional human being one but also the expectations and hegemonic discourses created by the source 'culture'. There is no such thing as a 'risk-free' translation when what is translated is problematic. However, my methodology proposes a solution that mitigates the problem. What may be achieved as a result is increased discussion and dialogue regarding both the issues discussed in source texts, through increased visibility of the translator, the translation process itself. On a shallow, idealist level, 'success' in the case of this project, where the translator is also the commissioner and is working freely, is achieving a translation that is 'accurate' and 'faithful' to the source text (ST) on a micro-textual level, thus meeting the purpose of scholarly, pedagogical translation. Any new 'controversies' that may arise as a result will need to be dealt with as they happen. Another condition for this particular project to be deemed as a success is a translation that may serve as an *unbiased* scholarly resource, one that is not likely to inflame further tensions. What differentiates this kind of project from other documentary translations can be attributed to the temporal nature of the undertaking.

DOI: 10.4324/9781003167792-5

As shall be discussed in more detail later, although something perhaps worth pursuing, complete mitigation of risk can never be truly guaranteed unless translation does not "happen" in the first place. Once again, we are reminded of the wise words of Grandpa Adam (if all else fails, prepare for the worst). The ideal of success in the sense of (relative) risk mitigation, would have to apply not only to the translator but also (amongst others), the ST author, commissioner (when there is one), and readership.

Philosophical Discussion – Key Questions

Before proceeding to concrete methodologies and the Compass of Translation, it would be wise to first addresses broad questions about translation and ethics, focusing first on the definition of 'controversy' itself, then discussing the management of risks potentially associated with the project. The broader, philosophical importance of translating controversial texts is addressed, before considering the best method for doing so.

Manga Kenkanryū has been deemed a 'racist' and 'acidic' work by critics in both Japan and South Korea (e.g., Itagaki, 2007a, 2007b; Sugiura, 2006/2007; Song, 2007; Kim, 2009), as well as overseas (e.g., White & Kaplan, 2006; Sakamoto & Allen, 2007; Liscutin, 2009). In order to answer this question of what exactly 'controversy' constitutes, I would first like to examine the definition the term itself. According to the *Marriam-Webster Dictionary of English* (2014) controversy is:

> [An] argument that involves many people who strongly disagree about something: strong disagreement about something among a large group of people . . . 1) a discussion marked especially by the expression of opposing views: DISPUTE 2) QUARREL, STRIFE.

Here, I would like to particularly note the use of the qualifier 'many people', for how can it be ascertained how such usage (plurality) came about and why? The issue of the dichotomy of the plural vs the singular is of importance, as in order to progress (to attempt to decide whether or not to translate), a translator should consider who represents whom in the relevant discourse. An important next step is to examine the etymology of the term: "Middle English *controversie*, from Anglo-French, from Latin *controversia*, from *controversus* disputable, literally, turned against, from *contro-* (akin to *contra-*) + *versus*, past participle of *vertere* to turn" (*Merriam-Webster Dictionary of English*, 2014). Evidently, the origins, the *traces* of how 'controversy' came to signify "strong disagreement among a *large group of* people" (*Merriam-Webster Dictionary of English*, 2014) have been lost to our definition. A question that comes to mind is what exactly constitutes a *large group* or even simply 'group'.

Juxtaposed against the context addressed in this book, historical and political issues between Japan and Korea, is it possible to proclaim that there are, within these two nations, large groups with opposing views, or is it simply a case of *a* minority versus *a* majority? In relative terms, Japanese and Korean right-wing activists may be downplayed and seen as a minority, but these are *groups of people* coming from a larger *whole* of society (emphasis on the singular nature of 'society'). Acknowledgement of this fact adds to the necessity for the translation of *Manga Kenkanryū*.

As is often the case, right-wing nationalists are the ones on whom focus is placed by the media, creating a certain representation of the *whole* of that society. The vicious circle of Japan-Korean relations, as addressed in my own research (Zulawnik, 2014), precisely points to such a phenomenon; negative views of Japan fuelled by Korean news coverage of *a* minority of right-wing politicians and activists, leading to broader anti-Japanese sentiment and, finally to close the circle, heated counter-attacks from anti-Korean groups in Japan. The point that I would like to make is that whilst definitions of controversy largely imply conflict between or within groups, it is often the case that these come to represent *a* whole. The parallel to be noted here is that the author and, when considering translation, the translator, also come to represent *the whole* – the author often on their own accord, the translator sometimes not. The very definition of controversy, therefore, requires reconsideration.

But is there an alternative, one that bypasses overlooking the individual? Controversy, I argue, stems from a loss of communication due to not only differing perceptions of events but also the actual way these events are referred to through language (and, finally, translation). This communication, however, is not in reference to a sudden formation of linguistic difference, such as may be imagined, for example, upon a literal interpretation of the outcome of the fall of the Tower of Babel. Communication issues are not always caused by language difficulty but also differing ideas and our understanding of concepts and signifieds. Translation and the translator, in this case, can play the role of a pedagogical tool or conduit in the furthering of knowledge, understanding, and, ultimately, dialogue. Communication issues are not always caused by language difficulty but can also stem from differing ideas. Considering current globalising trends, it is likely that the human race will one day return to being one group, the restoration of some perceived unity perhaps an ultimate, intrinsic goal. In the early 20th century, Count Richard Nikolaus von Coudenhove-Kalergi (Praktischer Idealismus, 1925) predicted ethnic groups eventually forming one, noting: "The Eurasian-Negroid race of the future, similar in its appearance to the Ancient Egyptians, will replace *the diversity of peoples with a diversity of individuals*" (p. 23, my emphasis). Von Coudenhove-Kalergi's (1925) prediction is of particular relevance to the point made above in regard to the imposed plurality of 'controversy' and resulting backlash on the representation of the singular whole. A 'diversity of individuals', thus, may be seen as a 'diversity of ideas', as a result of the coming together of the people. As 'controversial' as such a statement may now seem (for various reasons), it is not difficult to imagine such a 'coming together'. It may be centuries before the races become one in ethnic terms, perhaps many more when considering *langue*. What shall require the most time, however, is the road to the other unity aforementioned, that of accepting opposing ideas and 'individuality'. It is here that I propose a new definition for 'controversy', this wedge that split the peoples apart with the 'fall of Babel'. I propose this be done by the deconstruction of the term so that it reflects both on the concept of opposing ideas and, at the same time, unity and harmony – a necessary struggle for acceptance of the opposing truth.

Taking the first element of the word (as defined earlier), *contro-/contra-* I suggest *versus/vertere* be replaced with the derivative *'vers'* which, whilst still carrying the meaning of 'to turn' also relates to 'verse', defined as: "writing in which words are arranged in a rhythmic pattern" (*Merriam-Webster Dictionary of English*, 2014). Thus, controversy also comes to be read as *controvers* or *contravers*, meaning: a discourse where opposing ideas go in verse towards understanding. In other words, as opposed to controversy, where the nuance is negative and implicative of conflict, *controverse* stresses a positive outcome (at the end of controversy or chaos) in the form of *dialogue*. Addressing controversial issues is often a risky undertaking. Doing so through translation is no exception, which leads to the next question: what are the risks associated with translating controversial texts?

What Are the Risks?

The risks associated with translation, as discussed in the previous chapter, can be far reaching, something that is very relevant in the case of this project where the subject text is a source of controversy in Japan-South Korea relations. Translation risk can affect the translator, readership and, sometimes, even those not directly associated with the translation, as was illustrated in previous chapters. Those associated with translation, be it translators or commissioners, must, therefore, acknowledge this fact before proceeding with a project. Acknowledgment here carries both ethical and more practical significance, as shall be discussed later in the chapter.

Risks associated with the translation of a controversial text include creating new controversies, as well as aforementioned tangential risks that affect source text authors, such potential travel restrictions or prosecution. As mentioned in the book, the author has himself stated that he refused offers of a Korean translation of *Manga Kenkanryū* for the South Korean market upon advice from a lawyer that the venture could end with legal prosecution for anyone involved (Yamano, 2005). This is due to the existence of specific laws in South Korea banning any activities which may be deemed as anti-Korean or pro-Japanese. Apart from such tangible risks, the translation also risks continuing the controversy by rehearsing and spreading discourse that has been widely criticised as offensive.

Derrida's work has itself seen controversy and, in many ways, embodies the very concept. *Différance*, for example, or the idea of meaning differing/deferring in relation to adjacent modifiers, is evidence of the difficulty in not deeming something 'controversial' or debated. The translator's struggle in translating controversial terms found within this never-ending chain of signified-signifier and very often the end-result of this being completely overlooked by target readerships must, therefore, be acknowledged and dealt with appropriately by reintroducing the translator and inserting them into the chain. In other words, without falling victim to absolute relativism, one should acknowledge that risk can arise at any moment and/or situation as a result of modification or *différance*, whilst also striving to make this situation visible to the readership.

Why Should Controversial Texts Be Translated?

One of the key aspects of translating controversial texts is 'risk management'. Translators should be aware of potential risks, tangible or not, particularly when they are also the commissioners of a project, such as is the case here. The cognitive process of reviewing project risks allows the translator to make better translatorial decisions and, in the case of this project, the creation of a suitable methodology based on a clear pedagogical purpose. However, that still leaves debate about justification as to why controversial texts should be translated.

Translation, in the sense of pure language or *différance*, may be seen as a key tool in directing us to mutual understanding and acceptance, not through one language but through common ways of reading discourse. Translating controversial texts provides new potential for furthering understanding of 'the other'. The purpose of such a translation and the difficult decisions that must be made before the commencement of such a task may also be likened to the ideas of existentialist scholars such as Søren Kierkegaard and, later,

Karl Jaspers. Kierkegaard (1844) in his book *The Concept of Anxiety* illustrates the idea arguing that, whilst the thought of absolute freedom is terrifying, it is at the same time empowering in that it helps us become aware of our choices. This may be likened to the translator of the task at hand acknowledging their vast potential as information conduit and conforming to a carefully thought out, purpose specific translation approach. Thus, the translator in a task such as this is effectively an activist for dialogue and discussion through pedagogy.

Although not risk-free, the benefits of a translation such as that proposed as part of this project provide ample justification; the project aims to extend discussion on controversial topics through increased multilingual access to key texts found within relevant discourse (e.g., Japan-South Korea relations), as well as allowing for the development of a methodology that may be applied to other tasks such as translator training and text analysis.

Approach for Translating Controversy: The 'Compass of Translation'

Scholars in Translation Studies such as Venuti (e.g., 1995/2008), Gentzler (e.g., 1993), and Robinson (e.g., 1996), utilising readings of prominent thinkers such as Benjamin, Foucault, and Derrida, have over recent years come to favour strongly certain translation techniques that allow for the preservation of the 'other'. In *The Translator's Invisibility: A History of Translation*, advocating a foreignising approach as a "highly desirable . . . strategic cultural intervention", Venuti (1995/2008) asserts that translators should try and stray away from total domestication so as avoid invisibility (pp. 14–16). The concept of translator invisibility is a significant one, but perhaps not necessarily in the sense Venuti (1995/2008) would argue, claiming domestication (i.e., fluent translation) as dominating both British and American translation culture (p. 15). The idea that foreignisation, discussed earlier in this chapter, is an ethical translation strategy should be noted, with Venuti (1995/2008) stating that "domestication and foreignisation indicate fundamentally ethical attitudes towards a foreign text and culture, ethical effects produced by the choice of a text for translation and by the strategy devised to translate it" (p. 19). In the case of the project at hand, it is crucial to allow the receivers of the source culture to recognise the translated texts as translations through a fair representation of the ST and increased visibility of the translator is crucial. No matter how 'toxic' the source texts may seem to some, the approach that must be followed throughout the translation process is the maintenance of the 'foreignness' or 'otherness' of the originals through a certain amount of fidelity adjusted according to the project purpose, as exemplified in Chapter 5.

A foreignising approach to translation, for example, may be defined as generally constituting an emphasis on source text features through glossing, transliteration of ST terms, and inclusion of translator's notes. It would, however, be impractical to try to prescribe one micro-analytical, definite list of rules. Instead, the best approach would be to format a set of rules relevant to the current translation project, the aim of the latter half of this chapter. Above all, the most important step in achieving a pedagogical approach is rendering the methodology (and conduit or translator) visible to the target readership. Key concepts of this part of the methodology are based on the factors addressed in the previous part of this chapter, which may be summarised as: 1) understanding of, and reconciliation with, controversy or *contraverse*; 2) understanding and acceptance of project associated risks; 3) ethical justification for the translation of controversial texts as a means of achieving a pure language of mutual understanding and acceptance.

I have decided to term my approach 'The Compass of Translation'. As shall soon be discussed, the Compass of Translation is in fact none other than the translator themselves. Any methods are supplementary modes or functions stemming from the only real tool needed (one's own volition and action). It should be noted that, following the analysis of the importance of individualism in part one of this chapter, mention of the translator is in reference to *one*, the reason for which shall be addressed in more detail later.

Creating Dialogue Between Source Text, Translator, and Readership

The approach proposed in this project aims to foster critique on part of the readership achieved through recognition of the TT as a pedagogical translation. This interaction is achieved through increased visibility of the translator and translation, as well as supplementation of methodology for the translation of visual metaphors, both of which are only possible once the translator has been empowered and provided with the correct tools.

Empowering the Translator

The central figure of my argument in this book is the translator and, as has been discussed previously, there has been ample scholarship on empowering translators (e.g., Venuti, 1995/2008; Tymoczko, 2000; Tymoczko & Gentzler, 2002; Maier, 2007). Much of this research has focused on issues of cultural hegemony and how translators and translation may have an effect on minority cultures (Venuti, 1995/2008; Tymoczko & Gentzler, 2002; Maier, 2007). The empowerment proposed in this chapter, however, is a means of helping the translator *help others* make changes. Translation, whether it be inter or intra-linguistic, can aid in opening new dialogues through the increase of relevant resources. In other words, translation plays a crucial role in fostering communication. The translator of a project such as this should, thus, feel empowered, knowing that they are working towards increased discussion and mediation of all discourse, not just one particular agenda. The possession of this feeling of empowerment is vital in maintaining the push to engage in a translation that may otherwise appear too risky to work with. Rather than being a true ethical ideal or means of risk management, empowering the translator has largely been discussed as something that will eventually entail recognition.

Recognition, of course, is not always in monetary terms, (e.g., gaining recognition for having pursued a certain agenda may also bring satisfaction). The empowerment proposed in this chapter, on the other hand, is a means of helping the translator *help others* make changes. Translation itself is not the key to solving the world's problems in spite of having been portrayed by some in such a manner. Helping others make changes does not mean translation will solve any problems in and of itself. Having noted this, translation, whether it be inter- or intra-linguistic, can nevertheless aid in opening new dialogues through the increase of relevant resources. The translator of a project such as this should, thus, feel empowered, knowing that they are working towards increased discussion and mediation of all discourse, not just one particular agenda. As mentioned earlier, the act of such a translation itself is a form of activism aimed at fostering knowledge and learning; however, it must be conducted following certain guidelines.

Taking Responsibility – Precision in Guidance

Once the translator is empowered and aware of the responsibilities their 'new' power carries, there is a need to act. How can a translator guide the readership? The readership may be guided via the translator if they effectively serve the function of a 'compass of translation'. The translator should aim to guide the readership in understanding the source text including all the various implicit subtleties and, in the case of this translation, image. The translation of *Manga Kenkanryū*, for example, is aimed to serve a documentary and pedagogical function in the form of a scholarly resource. Translator visibility, discussed earlier, thus should be manifested in a different manner than in, for example, a novel, with the use of thorough, carefully composed translator's notes and additional commentary relating to images that may otherwise be misunderstood by the readership. In the context of literary translation, for instance, translator visibility may carry the aim of preserving a foreign culture through the use of a foreignising approach. As aforementioned, a foreignising approach may consist of any number of translation methods, including transliteration, foreign word usage, irregular grammar, and translator's notes. Special care must be taken, however, so as not to 'over-foreignise' or 'exoticise' the ST.

The suitability of the latter, translator's notes, annotation, or para-text (in the sense of elements other than the main body of text) in general, is debated, particularly when considering literary translation (e.g., Genette, 1997; Pellatt, 2013). Annotations carry a pedagogical function that may also in turn aid in risk mitigation through supplementation of, for example, ST terms otherwise potentially out of reach of the target readership (Delisle et al., 1999; Katan, 2018). The value of annotations is especially relevant in the case of documentary and scholarly translation and of particular importance considering the pedagogical nature of the project at hand. My stance in relation to translator's notes may, therefore, be seen as somewhat Nabokovian, although the approach is generally not so extreme as to contain more translator's notes than source text material (Nabokov, 1955/2012). Indeed, not all translator's notes are equal. For one, translator's notes may be objective or subjective and, in that sense, pose risks such as potential overuse of power by the translator (Pellatt, 2013). In the translation of historical documents, for example, translators (who often happen to also be historians) tend to express their own opinions on the ST discourse (e.g., Hou, 2014; Wu & Shen, 2014; Holton, 2014).

In the project at hand, translator's notes play multiple roles. In addition to informing readers about terms that are difficult to translate and providing information on certain cultural aspects found in the ST (Delisle et al., 1999), translator's notes are also used to make sure that readers, regardless of their source language ability, can understand and see the difficulties of reaching an appropriate set of meanings in a controversial context. In other words, translator's notes play a crucial function in giving additional visibility to the translator through an explicit exposition of the translation process. Thus, such notes may guide readers as to their appreciation of the many challenges faced by the translator during the translation process. From the perspective of the translator, this may also be seen as a form of risk mitigation.

As the compass of translation, the translator should aim to provide the readership with *precise* guidance as to their translation choices and what has/has not been brought over from the ST. The concept of the 'compass' also relates to the directional nature (different approaches) of translation, and guidance is in direct reference to this. The act of translation may be seen as consisting of a potentially limitless spectrum of approaches. There has been scholarship trying to map these approaches in relation to each other, and it is often the case that there exist dichotomies, some of which, indeed, have been discussed in earlier chapters. Although there is little certainty as to how these different approaches relate to each other, the idea that there almost always exists an alternative (opposing) direction is certain. Indeed, as mentioned earlier, even the act of *not* translating is counterbalanced.

Multi-dimensional Translation

In my proposed multi-dimensional approach, the empowered translator works to make the ST accessible for the target audience whilst maintaining visibility allowing for interaction among the readership and ST, TT, and translation process. The multi-modal nature of *manga* as a medium requires specific approaches for translation. A number of methods were tested in trying to overcome text-type related issues such as the translation of image. In the first approach, translated text was applied to scanned, edited images from the *manga*, a process involving the program Photoshop. Raw page scans from the comic were placed alongside translations. But this was found to have limitations and ethical pitfalls, as the process, for example, sometimes required the editing of ST image, particularly in the case of onomatopoeias and mimesis. The initial hypothesis was that English translations including visual editing for onomatopoeias would allow for greater appreciation and introduction of the source language. Furthermore, it was assumed that providing translator's notes at the end of the translation, as part of an appendix, would be the only viable option ensuring translator visibility, as well as understanding of the fact that what is being read is a translation. However, placing translator's notes at the end of the translation as part of an appendix led to target readership sometimes overlooking such paratextual elements, instead focusing on the visual nature of the medium, some readers commenting on how natural the pages looked and how the work was easy on the eyes.

These realisations led to further inquiry into translation techniques utilised in other media such as film, e-books, and online news articles. Of particular interest was the student-run news website *KoreaBang*, a website allowing readers to zoom over a translated body of text, which automatically then opens a pop-up box with the corresponding source text. Although the reasoning behind the approach is not made explicit, the fact that the website predominantly covers controversial news stories from South Korea and is run by graduates would suggest that it contains definite pedagogical and risk management orientated elements: the ability to access the source text allows for linguistic comparison and, for readers with source language ability, the option to check translation accuracy.

A similar practice that may be seen in translation in the audiovisual domain is subtitling as well as *fansubbing*, an amateur form of subtitling. Fansubbing is used to supplement the source message just like a translator's note would in a standard paper translation, but it carries certain constraints similar to those of the comic as well as others, such as temporal issues related to moving image (Cintas, 2012; Massidda, 2015).

The visibility afforded to the translator in a process such as was explored on the website allowed me to address the ethical pitfalls of translating controversial texts addressed earlier: it renders the process and the translator visible. Nevertheless, there are certain technological issues surrounding such an approach. The only readily available program allowing for the overlay of translated text is Great Manga Application Onidzuka (GMAO), an open source program largely used in unsolicited fan translation (e.g., scanlation – translation of scanned comics). It should be noted here that the didactic application of GMAO discussed within this book is an example of potential new usage. GMAO is a platform originally intended for the general translation of manga in a popular setting. Although it is not within the scope of the project to develop such resources and software, my work suggests that with specific adaptation for translation such technologies represent useful possibilities for the development of translation in the future.

The Potential of Emerging Technologies

Ideally, a program used in the translation of such materials would allow for indexing of translator input rendering the translation process transparent. This may include a developed interface with buttons allowing access to (turning on and off of) colour coded word categories such as speaker (as a literal approach may be more difficult to follow), translator's notes, and politically and/or historically controversial terms. The program GMAO, although promising in applications such as that proposed in this project, is not ideally suited for this type of translation as it currently does not allow for a full view of the TT page, meaning that readers must scroll down to see the bottom half of the page. This presentation changes the experience of the readers from that of seeing a full page of *manga* to seeing only part, which could potentially alter the subject of focus or even hinder contextual comprehension. However, it also has useful functions, such as access to the source text and ample space for translator's notes, as visible in the following examples.

The method of overlaying translation is exemplified and analysed through the presentation of examples pertaining to some of the key project ideas and issues, such as the translation of multi-modal material and controversial terms, as well as a full translation of *Hate Hallyu: The Comic* using GMAO, in order to demonstrate the potential for further development and pedagogical use of software that allows for the translation of multi-modal elements such as image.

Japanese-English Translation

The use of a program such as *GMAO* would aid in overcoming space constraint issues faced during the translation of the *manga* medium from Japanese into English. As much as 60% of the Japanese language is made up of highly compact Sino-Japanese words or Chinese character compounds (Jp. *jukugo*, 熟語; Shibatani, 1990). A Japanese source word made up of only two or three characters may thus, potentially, constitute twice as many target English words. The compact nature of some Japanese words poses problems when dealing with the translation of *manga*, as speech bubbles cannot be easily resized without manipulating surrounding images, something that may require author permission and is not always possible, impinging on the graphic presentation of the text.

Translators have used various methods to try and overcome space constraint issues when dealing with *manga*, utilising, for example, different font sizes and abbreviation (Zanettin, 2012). In the case of this project, where the translation is to serve a pedagogical purpose, accurate, non-abbreviated translation with detailed translator's notes is indispensable, both in providing the readership with clarification of controversial terms and making the translator and translation more visible. In addition, translator's notes pose a particularly difficult challenge when translating a multi-modal medium such as *manga*.

One option is to include in-text references to notes either located at the bottom of the page or in an appendix at the end of the text. Such placement of translator's notes is, however, not ideal, as placing translator's notes at the bottom of a page would require changing the page size or adding something new to the page, whilst an appendix would run the risk of being overlooked. A translation with an overlay such as is enabled by GMAO allows ample space for translator's notes and removes restrictions for translation length.

Multi-modal Aspects of Translation

The visual elements of *manga* or graphic novel, a multi-modal medium, are just as significant as text in the process of translation. Images may carry source text culture-bound elements with meaning or significance that is not immediately clear in target environments. Furthermore, the multi-modal nature of the medium adds to its value as a subject of research with multi-modal/comic translation gaining considerable attention in academia. The translation of metaphors and idioms is one of the most challenging tasks faced by translators. The methodologies for metaphor translation are relevant to both literary and non-literary translation and have been extensively discussed in translation studies, notably by Broeck (1978), Newmark (1981), Toury (1995), and, in more recent times, Schäffner (2012), based on earlier works by Lakoff and Johnson (1980).

In addition, *manga* contain visual metaphors requiring translation and/or reproduction. Visual metaphors often carry no textual cues and can be found in other visual media such cartoons and film. As part of the project, I propose a supplementation of metaphor translation methodology demonstrated through the usage of the program GMAO. Doing so, I argue that visual metaphor translation is especially troublesome, as it can often be difficult to determine the extent to which an image is culture bound. Furthermore, the task can be made all the more challenging when translating controversial texts such as the subject of this project. The idea visually portrayed by the author can easily become hyper or under-translated, potentially resulting in misinterpretation on the part of the readership.

The implementation of the program *GMAO* helps the translator by allowing analysis of image without its modification. Normally when translating a visual metaphor, a translator would either have to resort to a note (for which there may be limited or no space) or even abandon the task, hoping the ST meaning is understood by the target audience. With a program such as GMAO, which allows for the temporary overlay of text, a translator could provide an explanation of said metaphor.

Hate Hallyu: The Comic contains a number of pages that may be deemed to be multi-modal. An example is found on page 149 from the second volume of the series, where one of the main characters appears on a motorcycle in the dream of the protagonist dressed in a uniform reminiscent of that of a Nazi SS officer. The character wears an arm band reading "Human Rights Officer" and orders the arrest of the protagonist. The image is presumably used to argue against 'extreme political correctness', the Nazi-like officer representing extreme measures. Such a semiotic shorthand may be likened to the popularised expression 'grammar Nazi', denoting someone who ruthlessly corrects others on their grammar mistakes. The use of such a multi-modal element may not be easily comprehensible even to the source

Figure 5.1 Manga Kenkanryū 2, p. 149 (Yamano, 2006)

readership, but it is here that the translator has the ability to aid in further understanding of the text.

Through the use of a program such as GMAO, the translator is able to provide a detailed opinion as to the meaning of a multi-modal element such

Figure 5.2 Hate Hallyu: The Comic 2, p. 149, via GMAO

as that illustrated earlier, without having to modify the image or be limited by strict space constraints as those mentioned earlier. Figure 5.2 is an example of what a translation of this example would look like after having been translated using GMAO.

The reader is able to switch views from the translation/translator's note to the raw ST image, allowing for closer analysis of the original and translation. The ability to switch from ST to TT is also beneficial for the translation of controversial or difficult terms, as shall be discussed in the following section.

Translating Controversial Terms

As a graphic novel aimed at Japanese adults interested in Japan-South Korea relations, *Hate Hallyu: The Comic* contains numerous historical and political terms, some of which contain more than one English equivalent or existing translation. The issue of selection here is important, as some choices may be directly linked to what often sparks 'controversy', thus raising risk.

Translator's notes (TN) and GMAO play a big role in helping manage risk by allowing the translator to explain, to the best of their ability, issues pertaining to certain choices, whilst also allowing for the creation of new, alternative translations. The ability to have a new translation side by side with translator's notes (as made possible with GMAO) explaining background issues regarding terminology, therefore, has some pedagogical significance. The decision to include TNs for such terms was made on the basis that the target audience may wish to further investigate the issues.

Another relevant example is the term *kōminka seisaku* (Jp. 皇民化政策), translated here as 'Imperialisation of the People policy', a calque translation (Delisle et al., 1999). Although this term is often translated into English as either *Japanisation*, *Tennōisation*, or *assimilation* (*kōminkaseisaku*, 2012), each choice is problematic: *Japanisation* can be seen as considerably Eurocentric, as the concept of assimilation into empire is certainly not exclusive to Japan, whilst *Tennōisation* is a term derived from *tennō*, the Japanese word for *emperor* and not *kōmin* (emperor's people). When compared with *Nazification*, a similar term, *Tennōisation* is in fact illogical and inaccurate in terms of lexical composition. Whereas Nazification (*Nazi + fication*) makes sense in that it is *making something/someone Nazi*, *Tennōisation* (*tennō + isation*) literally means *turning something/someone into the Emperor of Japan*. When back-translated into Japanese (Jp. *tennōka*, 天皇化), the term makes just as little sense. Neither are terms that Japanese characters in *Hate Hallyu: The Comic* would use. Finally, *assimilation*, another lexical option, is on the other side of the spectrum, too broad with no reference to *empire* and thus not in line with the general foreignising approach utilised as part of this project.

From the perspective of a Japanese person coming in contact with the term *kōminka seisaku*, it is likely that the image that first comes to mind is that of a people becoming part of a/the 'Japanese Empire' or 'the Emperor's people'. Indeed, the term is often defined as such in Japanese dictionaries:

A Japanese occupational policy from World War II which colonised Korea [*chōsen*] as part of wartime mobilisation. Under the name of "cultural assimilation" it was aimed at making Koreans loyal people of the [Japanese] Emperor, whilst obliterating national identity. The policy included name change [*sōshikaimei*] and educational regulations [*kyōikurei*] [my translation].

(The Great Japanese Dictionary, 1995, p. 741)

Thus, it is hard to imagine a Japanese reader envisioning *kōminka seisaku* as a policy that *Japanises*, *Tennōises* (?), or simply *assimilates* a people. Furthermore, *Japanisation* and *Tennōisation* may both be seen as orientalist terms that were coined for a non-Japanese, anglophone readership reading in a context that purely focuses on Japanese imperialism, making both terms exclusive to that particular setting. Nevertheless, all three terms, *Japanisation*, *Tennōisation*, and *assimilation*, have been mentioned in the TNs for reference, as they are commonly used terms when referring to the concept of *kōminka seisaku*.

A further, politically significant term, often raised by those involved in Japan-South Korea relations and the issue of wartime reparations/ compensation/apologies, is the very ST term for compensation and repara- tion, *hoshō* (Jp. 補償) and *tsugunai* (Jp. 償い). Official Japanese govern- ment ST documents use both terms, the latter also carrying the meaning of *atonement* (for wrongdoings). Organisations arguing that Japan did not provide sufficient compensation or that the compensation was not 'heart- felt' tend to render both terms simply as (financial) *compensation*. Parties that, on the other hand, argue that Japan has done everything it needs to, argue that *tsugunai* indeed refers to both compensation and atonement, thus "no further apologies from the government are required". This translation project does not aim to argue that translators are to determine which party is 'correct'. Rather, the aim is to argue that one function a translator may wish to offer is the provision of access to detailed translations of controver- sial terms, so that third parties may reach a more complete or sophisticated understanding of the finer points of certain debates.

Foreignisation – An Ideal 'Direction' for Controversy?

It is now my intention to juxtapose some of these approaches in the form of a compass, which may be seen as an aid in visualising the dynamic nature of the translation task (cf. *Figure 5.3* below). Through such a visualisation, a translator may be better equipped in guiding the readership as to their translation choices. In order to maintain project scope, I shall only focus on the dichotomy of foreignisation vs domestication, although the compass may also be utilised to map other translation approaches. It should also be noted that the compass of translation should be visualised as being three dimensional – a sphere, at the (arbitrary) centre of which lies discourse. The concept of discourse and its value in this instance may be seen as parallel to that described by Derrida – it is effectively "neutral" in relation to the direc- tions in which the modifying being, in this case the translator, shall take it. Thus, a source text may be racist or humorous, but, in relation to the transla- tion task and possible translation approaches, it is all there is to begin with.

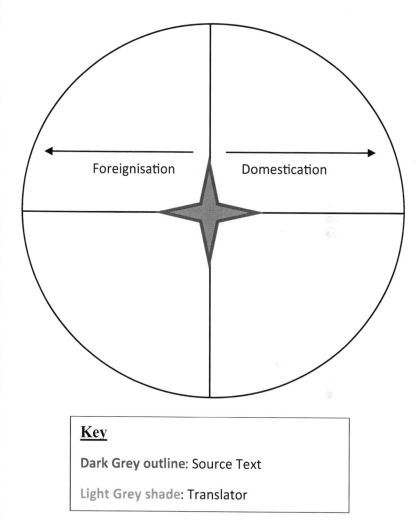

Figure 5.3 The Compass of Translation, Foreignisation vs Domestication

Embodied with the ST is the empowered translator, a translator who has already made the decision to translate the chosen ST. It is the translator's task, their will, to modify (translate) the ST in certain ways (by following certain approaches) so as to make it accessible for the target audience. As has been mentioned throughout this chapter, just how this translator/ translation shall be received is decided largely upon the current portrayal and reception of the ST. It is therefore not so much *how* a text is translated, but *what* is being translated that orchestrates third parties' opinions of the translator and, more importantly, risk factors.

Moving as one, the translator and ST begin to change. The directions the translator decides to follow are not limited to one bearing. A translator will go back and forth, following many angles (foreignising, domesticating, translating literally, glossing, etc.), although here it should be noted that it is theoretically possible to follow 'one route' to the very end, contrary to popular belief. The dichotomy of foreignisation vs domestication has been deemed part of a continuum by scholars such as Basil Hatim, and yet, when visualising the different paths on the compass of translation, it possible to say that there is a point where a text 'returns' to the starting point. This is an important concept as it brings weight to the argument and justification for a foreignising approach in certain circumstances.

When a ST is translated using a foreignising approach, the resulting TT will always (to varying extent) bear increased resemblance with the ST. So much so, in fact, that if a translator were to continuously follow a foreignising 'direction' the translation would eventually return to the form of the ST – the point of departure. Remembering that the compass is a sphere, one can see that following any particular axis will eventually lead back to the same point. A foreignising approach brings the text closer to itself (to the original). This is a polarising effect, as whilst the translation becomes increasingly foreign for the readership, it also becomes increasingly domesticated from the point of view of the source culture. In the case of Japanese or Korean translation, for example, complete foreignisation would end in the Romanisation of the ST and, following this, translation of the Romanised text back into the Japanese or Korean writing system. Paradoxically, the result would still, technically, be a 'translation' due to its 'journey'. Conversely, a domesticating approach would eventually lead to a text hardly resembling that of the original. The resulting text would instead seem completely foreignised from the perspective of the source culture, which may be seen as inappropriate for the purpose of this project as the readership are to achieve as much exposure as possible to key features of the ST.

Summary

I have chosen to redefine the term 'controversy' and re-conceptualise it so as to incorporate Deconstructionist ideas of reading and trying to make sense of discourse. Likewise, I have chosen to take the time to discuss risk factors directly relating to the project at hand in light of both physical (mortal risk) and metaphorical aspects with emphasis on the unavoidable (con)textual risks so as to allow for a more tangible example of the realities of 'controversial translation'. Factors surrounding the text pose significant risk that may be discussed in relation to whether or not anything can in fact be achieved in terms of traditional risk management. Whilst I argue that little can be done to eliminate translation related risks as risk is governed more by the ST than how a translation is carried out, what may be achieved is a clear purpose and project justification – increased discussion about controversial discourse with the hope of attaining increased understanding through discussion.

I note that although full safety (zero risk) would only be achievable if a translation did not happen in the first place, there are methods that may help lower risk factors. It is with this that I propose applying a methodological framework to translating as a 'visible and aware guide'. The translator has the power to supplement the ST and potentially mislead the readership, thus I would argue that there is a need to provide guidance to the readership in the form of detailed, unbiased translator's notes that also may then aid in terms of risk management. I propose the application of a methodological framework termed the *Compass of Translation*. Here it was noted that the *Compass of Translation* is in fact the translator as they have the power to supplement the ST and, conversely, potentially mislead the readership (intentionally or not). I argue that the translator should provide guidance to the readership in the form of detailed, unbiased translator's notes that also have the function of risk management. The visual nature of the Compass of Translation is significant, as it may be applied to the mapping of translation approaches.

The final part of the framework addresses the translator playing the role of a guide to the translation process. This function may be exemplified using the binary most relevant to the project at hand; foreignisation vs domestication. I argue that a foreignising approach is most appropriate in achieving the translation purpose, as by following this direction the translator is moving closer towards the ST. The suitability of a foreignising may be further strengthened through the reconsideration of our view on the dichotomy itself, as continually foreignising a text would eventually lead back to the ST (thus meaning foreignisation and domestication do not form a perfect continuum as once thought) and is in line with Berman (1985/2012) as well as Bassnett and Lefevere's (1990) argument regarding foreignisation's potential pitfalls when taken to the extreme ('exoticisation').

My proposed methodological approach for the translation of controversial documents may be summarised as follows:

1   Recognition of the translation as a scholarly one with a pedagogical purpose. The aim of the translation is not to comment on discourse but to allow for the discussion of debated issues as a means of working towards a meta-language of mutual acceptance of the individual thinker.

2   Recognition and understanding of translator power and associated responsibility. Translators working out of their own commission have power to modify a text in any number of ways, but some approaches are more suitable than others depending on the purpose. A purpose such as the one pertaining to the project at hand (cf. point one) requires restraint of this power, shown through a provision of guidance for the readership.

3   Commitment to guiding the readership through understanding of the *Compass of Translation* and use of notations or programs such as GMAO. Guidance should be provided using detailed, carefully thought-out translator's notes/annotations that: 1) supplement the reader's factual/cultural knowledge and 2) illustrate and justify the translator's decision making. Justification through the use of translator's notes as part of the multi-dimensional approach discussed in this chapter may also play a role in risk management as there is less chance of the readership mistaking the translator as somehow agreeing or disagreeing with the ST message. Guidance should also be provided using a detailed preface justifying reasons behind the choice of text and approach.

4   Recognition and acknowledgment of ethical and risk-related factors in relation to all parties concerned. What may be some of the potential negative outcomes of the translation? The decision to translate, if made out of one's own volition/agency, should be done with careful consideration of various contextual factors and based upon common sense. Risks should only be taken at the translator's (carefully deliberated and informed) discretion.

6 Case Study

Translating *Manga Kenkanryū*

Following the methodology and framework proposed in this book, this section seeks to exemplify the resulting approach through a case study. The first section focuses predominantly on broader issues concerning the overall translation approach, the selected medium and inherent stylistics, and paratextual elements. It addresses the intrinsic issues that arose throughout the translation process so as to maintain the chosen methodology. The medium, in this case the Japanese graphic novel (*manga*), manifests certain stylistic and paratextual qualities such as varying levels of politeness in speech and sometimes culturally bound imagery including, for example, visual metaphors. Part two provides chapter-specific, lexicological analysis, organised in chapter-order, thus taking into account a majority of the nine chapters in the publication. The structure of this chapter, whilst divided into sections as per the chapters in *Manga Kenkanryū/Hate Hallyu: The Comic*, identifies key themes that are shared across the publication, and it is framed by initial analysis if issues of style and visual (multi-modal) translation.

General Issues: Translating *Manga*

As discussed earlier in the book, translating graphic novels carries medium-specific challenges, the greatest perhaps the transformation of culture-bound paratextual elements such as image (cf. e.g., Leppihalme, 1994; Jüngst, 2008; Zanettin, 2008; Pasfield-Neofitou & Sell, 2016). Translating image poses problems for the translator as it often involves the use of some form of technology and working with or without cooperation/permission from the original author (an issue of ethics). Indeed, the main issues during the translation of *Manga Kenkanryū* involved the translation of image and context found in a controversial text. The proposed approach for the translation of controversial materials and, in that, visual media such as the graphic novel, involves the use of technology in the form of the computer program GMAO. Doing so allows for more translator-reader interaction via translator's notes that exist in the same dimension as the source text (ST)

DOI: 10.4324/9781003167792-6

and may be toggled on/off at the discretion of the reader. Such an approach offers pedagogical benefits, as it renders the translation process transparent: readers are given constant access to the ST as well as detailed translator commentary where appropriate. This offers the benefit of readers being able to learn about cultural elements that are image-bound as has been discussed by Cohn (2013) in relation to teaching translation and language through the use of image.

In the least, in cases where the translator feels the translation may be inadequate or there is risk of misunderstanding, it allows for the inclusion of thorough translator's notes that may otherwise not be an option due to space restrictions inherent to the medium. As a result of such space restrictions, translator's notes often have to be attached as part of an appendix where there is always a risk they will be overlooked.

As argued throughout this project, as well as serving a highly educational process, such interaction may also to some extent protect the translator and the author in that there is less room for misunderstanding the translation purpose or mistaking the translation as a standalone text, separate from the ST.

Style: Text, Tone, and Character Voices

One of the issues faced throughout this particular translation was the appearance of an array of speech types and levels. A feature of the Japanese language is the distinction between various levels of formality in speech that may be marked through the use of different lexicon (such as nouns and verbs).

Formal language (*teineigo/teineitai*, Jp. 丁寧語・丁寧体), which can then be largely divided into honorific and humble language (*keigo* and *kenjōgo*, Jp. 敬語・謙譲語), is contrasted by plain language (*futsūtai*, Jp. 普通体) and, in case of more informal speech, *tameguchi* (Jp. ため口). The usage of the different speech levels is dictated by a broad range of factors such as age, social standing, and familiarity of the speakers. *Manga Kenkanryū* is no exception, with characters who find themselves in various social settings using different forms. It is through this contextual language usage that readers of the Japanese ST are able to recognise quickly the different relationships present within the dialogue (Akamatsu, 2011). The main protagonist, Kaname Okiayu, for example, exclusively uses formal language when communicating with his university senior (Jp. *senpai*, 先輩), as well as using the honorific suffix *san* (Jp. さん).[1]

The method used in translating honorific suffixes varies according to the translation purpose. The purpose of the project at hand is to create a pedagogical translation that may be used for further enquiry into the subject matter as well as the process of translation itself, and the translator's reasoning. I chose, thus, to employ a considerably foreignising approach that may be seen in the retention of the aforementioned honorific suffixes, with the addition of translator's notes outlining meaning and usage. Although the English language does not have perfectly corresponding equivalents for much of the Japanese honorific language, a similar contrast may be achieved through the use of varying speech levels, marked by, for example, contractions. The first example of mixed speech levels may be seen on page 45 in Chapter 2 of *Manga Kenkanryū*. Kaname and his girlfriend Itsumi attend their first debate after signing up for one of their university's historical circles, the Far East Asia Investigation Committee. The committee is led by Sueyuki Ryūhei, a university senior. The young couple switch between informal language for dialogue between themselves/self-talk and formal language in reference to Sueyuki as well as the opposing debate team:

ST: 末行さん、向こう明らかにオバサンとオッサンばっかり じゃないですか!?
  TT: Sueyuki-san, are not the other party clearly old folks!?

Source: (Japanese ST) *Manga Kenkanryū*, (English TT) *Hate Hallyu: The Comic*, p. 45

The Japanese honorific suffix *san* is retained, with the addition of the following translator's note laid over the corresponding Japanese term. The note is shown the first time *-san* appears in the comic (p. 35):

TN: '-san' (Jp. san, さん) is an honorific suffix attached at the end of names in Japanese to denote factors such as hierarchy. In this instance, Sueyuki Ryūhei is Okiayu Kaname and Aramaki Itsumi's senior.

Source: Hate Hallyu: The Comic (via *GMAO*), p. 35

Similarly, other nuanced forms of language like verb endings used by senior characters such as the protagonist's grandfather or characters from a certain perceived social class may be substituted by contextual English equivalents. A good example of such substitution may be seen in Chapter 2, where Kaname is participating in a heated debate about post-war reparations. The other party to the debate, the so-called 'pro-citizens', contains a middle-aged female member who uses the verb ending *zamasu* (Jp. ざます), which is often associated with wealthy and 'arrogant' female speakers from the Tokyo area (Katō, 2000):

ST: ざます
   TT: Goody

Source: (Japanese ST) *Manga Kenkanryū*, (English TT) *Hate Hallyu: The Comic*, p. 44

Although there is no direct equivalent for the verb ending *zamasu*, a similar effect was achieved by using *goody* (and later, on page 65, *if I must say so*) which, although archaic, is often associated in English with the 'high-class'. It should be noted that *zamasu* itself is archaic, with most modern usage seen in satirical contexts. Thus, *goody/if I must say so* may not be a perfect equivalent for *zamasu*, nevertheless it brings attention to the particular character's (intentional) 'quirky' feature present in the ST. In addition to this, the GMAO version of the TT would also include a translator's note detailing the ST feature as follows:

TN: The ST uses the verb ending '*zamasu*' which, traditionally pertaining to high-class Yamanote dialect (*Shōgakukan Gendai Reikai Kokugo Jiten*, 2011), tends to be associated with affluent females from the Tokyo region. The verb ending is uncommon in general usage and may be seen as a tool used in satire. For example, in popular contexts, such as manga, characters portrayed as being affluent (and often, as a result, also arrogant), may be seen using this verb ending, an example being Sune'o's mother from the anime *Doraemon*.

Source: Hate Hallyu: The Comic (via *GMAO*), p. 65

As outlined in earlier chapters, the aim and function of the translator's notes is bifold. They are predominantly used:1) to inform the readers about the meaning of culturally/linguistically bound ST items that may otherwise be misunderstood and 2) to make the translation and, as a result, the translator visible. As aforementioned, this method has pedagogical applications – it renders the translation process transparent whilst also allowing for a clear distinction between the ST and TT, at the same time potentially resulting in risk minimisation. Special care is taken to supplement translation choices perceived as troublesome, not only with translator's notes but also relevant references to other sources, as illustrated by the previous example.

Apart from the character tone issue discussed earlier, another general issue faced during the translation process was the transliteration of proper names. The issue carries greater importance than in a translation of an uncontroversial source, as it is vital to allow readers to be able to have a more accurate idea about who or what is being discussed. This accuracy is particularly important when dealing with the names of politicians and other well-known figures. Although presented as a text about 'fictional characters' (Yamano, 2004) *Manga Kenkanryū* lists the names of numerous real-life public figures from Japanese and Korean politics, media, and history. When translating names, the choice was made to provide the most popular Romanisation available. In case a popular English Romanisation is unavailable, the choice was made to use the most popular Romanisation system (Hepburn Romanisation and Revised Romanisation of Korea for Japanese and Korean, respectively), with the English name-surname order. An example of this resolution may be seen below:

Table 6.1 Translation of names in *Hate Hallyu: The Comic*

Source Text	Hepburn Transcription	Target Text
沖鮎要	Okiayu Kaname	Okiayu Kaname
李浩明	Ri Kōmei	Ho-Myeong Lee
李承晩	Ri Shōban/I Sunman	Rhee Syngman
蒋介石	Shō Kaiseki	Chiang Kai-Shek

As shown in the table, the main protagonist's name (Kaname Okiayu) has been translated using the standard Hepburn system, with the surname-name order kept as in the ST. In the case of the Korean/Japanese politician Ho-Myeong Lee, the only available source is the ST Chinese character name, which under the Hepburn system would be Romanised as Ri Kōmei. As the name is originally Korean, the choice was made to translate using Revised Romanisation of Korean. The justification behind this choice was readability – whereas most Japanese ST readers know that 'Ho-Myeong Lee' comes from a Korean background not only based on the context but also the name in Chinese characters ('Lee' being a common Korean surname), TT English background readers may think otherwise if the name was to be Romanised as *Ri Kōmei*. Similarly, with *Syngman Rhee*, most Japanese readers identify the politician based on the Chinese character name. The task of such identification would be much more troublesome for TT readers had *Ri Shōban*, *I Sunman*, or even *Seungman Lee* been used in place of *Syngman Rhee*, as the latter is the standard Romanised variation used in literature and by the politician himself. The final example in Table 6.1 is that of Chiang Kai-Shek, who is mentioned briefly on page 81 (Chapter 3), of the *manga*. As with the Syngman Rhee example, TT readers would have trouble recognising *Shō Kaiseki*, so the choice was made to use the most known variation in the Anglophone world – *Chiang Kai-Shek*.

Apart from the names of well-known figures and other characters present in the *manga*, a challenging aspect was the translation of *Korea* itself. As the topics in *Manga Kenkanryū* largely pertain to *Korea*, translating the variations present in the text took on profound importance. Languages that contain words derived from Chinese such as Japanese and Korean have more than one term for what is generally translated in English simply as *Korea*. These variations carry their own political implications and deeply impinge on the perceptions of the general populations of Japan and South/North Korea.

As outlined in section 2.1, the Korean Peninsula has seen great unrest in the past century, transforming from a Kingdom to an Empire, then a Japanese colony and, finally, the two separate states of the present day. It is paramount to keep in mind this history when dealing with translation pertaining to Japan-Korea relations, as in a translation with a pedagogical purpose such as this (creation of a research source) there should be well-balanced, informative translator's notes that do not try to persuade the readership in any particular direction, allowing for further, independent research on the subject matter.

There exist two general terms for 'unified Korea' in Japanese and Korean when written using Chinese characters; *Chōsen/Joseon* (Jp/Kr. 朝鮮) and *Kankoku/Hanguk* (Jp. 韓国, Kr. 韓國), respectively. The former, *Chōsen/Joseon*, was used in both Japan and Korea (prior to division) to refer to the kingdom and, with the addition of *peninsula*, to the *Korean Peninsula* as well. When the Korean Empire was established in 1897, the formal name was changed to *Daikan-teikoku/Daehan- jeguk* (Jp. 大韓帝国, Kr. 大韓帝國), the *Kan/Han* character being used for the first time in Korea in thousands of years. There is debate as to the origins and usage of *Daikan/Daehan*, with some scholars such as Choe Nam-Seon (1946) arguing that the two characters when used together phonetically trace their root back to an ancient word simply meaning "person who lives in the area that is now the south of the Korean Peninsula", as opposed to *Dai/Dae* being a glorifying adjective meaning *big* or *great*, as in 'Great Korea'. At the time of the establishment of the empire, however, Japan, by far the biggest force in East Asia (and, as discussed in the historical background chapter, arguably a driving force in both the formation and downfall of the Korean Empire), also used the same character in front of *Japan* to mean *Great Japanese Empire* (Jp. *Dai-Nihon*

Teikoku, 大日本帝国). The variations present in *Manga Kenkanryū* and their proposed English translations may be summarised as follows:

Table 6.2 Comparison of 'Korea' related translation choices

Source Text	Target Text
韓・韓民族	Korea/the Korean people
韓国	South Korea/Republic of Korea (ROK)
嫌韓流	Hate Hallyu
韓国人・韓国語/朝鮮語	South Korean/Korean (language)
北朝鮮	North Korea/Democratic People's Republic of Korea (DPRK)
朝鮮・朝鮮人	Joseon Korea/Joseon Korean
朝鮮半島	Joseon Peninsula

When the Korean Empire then became part of the Japanese Empire in 1910, the name of the region reverted back to *Chōsen/Joseon*. Then, after the end of World War Two and the Korean War, the peninsula was divided into the North and South, both factions choosing to use different official names based on their political ideologies. The different names used for *Korea* and the *Korean Peninsula* may be summarised as follows:

Table 6.3 Comparison of naming of 'Korea'

English	Japanese[2]	North Korean	South Korean
Korea (general)	韓国・朝鮮 *Kankoku/Chōsen*	조선 (朝鮮) *Joseon*	한국 (韓國) *Hanguk*
Korean Peninsula	朝鮮半島 *Chōsen Hantō*	조선반도 (朝鮮半島) *Joseon Bando*	한반도 (韓半島) *Han-Bando*
North Korea (DPRK)	朝鮮人民共和国・北朝鮮 *Chōsen Minshushugi Jinmin Kyōwakoku/ Kita-Chōsen*	조선인민공화국/북조선 (朝鮮人民共和國/北朝鮮) *Joseon Minjujuwi Inmin Gonghwaguk/ Buk-Joseon*	북한 (北韓) *Buk-Han*
South Korea (ROK)	大韓民国・韓国 *Daikan minkoku/Kankoku*	남조선 (南朝鮮) *Nam-Joseon*	대한민국/한국/남한 (大韓民國/韓國/南韓) *Daehan minguk/ Hanguk/ Nam-Han*

The communist North (DPRK) chose to retain the pre/post-imperial era *Chōsen/Joseon* (adding *Democratic People's Republic*), whilst the South (ROK) took the *Daikan/Daehan* from imperial times (adding *minkoku/minguk*, meaning *republic*).[3] When referring to one another, the DPRK and ROK opt to use their own selected name, with the addition of North/South for disambiguation. In other words, in the DPRK North and South Korea are called *Buk-Joseon/Nam-Joseon* (北朝鮮・南朝鮮), with the peninsula referred to as the *Joseon Bando* (朝鮮半島). In contrast to this, in South Korea, the North and South are referred to as *Buk-Han* and *Nam-Han* (北韓・南韓), with the peninsula referred to as the *Han-Bando* (韓半島). The same is the case for most adjectival usage, such as in language (Kr. *Joseon-mal* versus *Hanguk-mal*) and the Korean ethnicity (N. Kr *Joseon-minjok* versus S. Kr *Han-minjok*). What complicates matters further is third-party naming. In non-Sino-background languages, both *Joseon* and *Han* are known simply as *Korea*, as in the *Korean Peninsula*, *Korean language*, and *Korean people*. A distinction can only be made with the addition of North/South, but this is rarely done and does not come of help when dealing with *Korea* prior to division. In Sino-background languages such as Chinese, Japanese, and Vietnamese, there is a balance in usage, with each state referred to using its preferred name and the Korean Peninsula as the *Joseon Peninsula* (using each language's respective pronunciation), in other words, using the historical reference of the peninsula prior to division.

The multiplicity of terms is a problem when translating, as the usage of either of the two terms, namely, *Joseon Peninsula* or *Han Peninsula*, is not recognised by the opposing faction. On the contrary, the use of, for example, *Chōsen Hantō* (*Joseon Peninsula*) in Japanese is often met with distaste from South Korea as it is perceived as a reminder of Japanese Imperial rule. Prominent figures in South Korean society such as Im Jong-Geon, ex-president of *Seoul Gyeongje* newspaper, even argue that the Japanese usage of the term 'in place' of the South Korean variant may be seen as sympathetic to North Korea or as taking pride in Japanese colonial history (Im, 2015).

At first, discussing the translation of lexicon such as *Korea* in languages other than those predominant in the ST and TT (e.g., Korean) may seem irrelevant. An important point, however, is the multicultural nature of the ST. Whilst many of the characters in *Manga Kenkanryū* are shown as being of a Korean ethnic background, one may argue that their Japanese language usage within the text differs from that normally expected. Vocal, Zainichi (Japan resident) South Korean characters, for example, still refer to the Korean Peninsula as the *Joseon Peninsula* (Jp. *chōsen hantō*, 朝鮮半島) and the Korean race as the *Joseon people* (Jp. *chōsen minzoku*, 朝鮮民族) which, whilst standard for most Japanese speakers, is not a likely vocabulary choice under such circumstances in reality. Whilst Yamano does try to emulate such detail (vocal Zainichi Korean characters such as Kōichi generally refer to Korea, regardless of time period, as *kankoku* – South Korea), this usage is not perfect, and there are, as aforementioned, a number of contradicting areas. As a translator with knowledge of the Japanese and Korean languages, as well as the situation surrounding language use in certain circles, I contend that there is a need to provide additional detail pertaining to such ST features. It must be noted, however, that in the case of this project purpose it is not my intent to guide TT readers to any particular conclusion regarding the ST. The project purpose is to create a research resource, with addition of information in the form of didactic translator's notes. Ultimately, whether or not this has been carried out properly will be decided by the readers, and the exercise of trying to translate for such a purpose carries further pedagogical value. When translating a text for pedagogical purposes, such as in the case of this project, a choice has to be made as to what to do with politically charged terms, not so much as to appease either side of the divide but how to (or *if to*) highlight the existence of this 'différance' (cf. Chapter 4). Whatever the language may be, every reader (native or not) has the potential to (mis)understand a text in any given way.

A translator must then assume that there is a certain, 'general' habitual understanding/knowledge common to, for example, Japan and the "general" Japanese public. This assumption does not, however, solve the problem of translation, as the translator and the envisaged target readership have to be accounted for as well. Thus, as discussed in the methodology chapter, just as there is no 'total equivalence', there is no 'neutral' or 'perfect' translation. The aim of this project, however, is to propose new methods of engaging with this 'impossible' task. In other words, the purpose is to allow the target readership to see the many dimensions to understanding a text, through the translation process. This understanding, in turn, may allow for deeper insight into the complexity of controversial issues, such as Japan-Korea relations, ultimately leading to further research and dialogue.

Apart from issues of register and voice and the translation of politically and contextually significant proper nouns, particular attention was paid to text-type differences present within the volume of *Manga Kenkanryū*. Although the majority of the *manga* is in standard format (written by Yamano), the volumes also contain a number of formal articles written by notable right-wing figures such as Kanji Nishio, president of the Japanese Society of History Textbook Reform (Jp. *Atarashii Rekishi Kyōkasho wo Tsukuru Kai*, 新しい歴史教科書をつくる会) and Masao Shimojō, Professor of International Development at Takushoku University, presumably for the purpose of supporting argumentation with 'real-world research'. The tone used in these articles is very different from that of the rest of the *manga*. The style is formal, and there are no paratextual elements such as images. The authors are introduced in detail at the beginning of each article, listing credentials as well as references to other relevant publications. The tone of the TT was translated so as to match that of the ST – in other words, the translation was carried out according to text-type, with the use of GMAO allowing target readers to have immediate visual access to the change in layout. Additional attention was paid to the different writing styles exhibited by the featured authors. As is the case with any language, writing style can vary greatly according to the individual.

In the case of *Manga Kenkanryū*, all four 'columns' provided by the authors other than Yamano differ in writing style. The first article by Kanji Nishio (pp. 98–102), an honorary professor at the University of Electro-Communications, Tokyo and political commentator, is written using a largely formal, academic tone. A determining feature is the systematic usage of the plain-form verb *dearu* (Jp. である) which is most commonly used in scholarly exposition, the style also known as *dearu-tai* (Jp. である体). There is no emotive language, contractions, or slang, the absence of which has been reproduced in the English translation.

The second article, by writer and political commentator Kōyū Nishimura (pp. 175–178), although also written in plain form, is less formal than the article by Nishio. As opposed to *dearu-tai* the article is written using *da-tai*, which is more common in journalistic articles. The language conventions utilised in Nishimura's article include rhetorical devices giving the piece a more reflective feel when compared to that of Nishio. Although the translator's notes applied to these particular articles do not include explanation of every literary device used, there is a brief general summary of overall form, as in the following example:

TN: The source text article is written almost exclusively in *dearu-tai* (Jp. である体), a form most commonly seen in formal writing such as academic articles. The form's name originates from the simple-verb form *dearu* (En. 'to be/is').

Source: Hate Hallyu: The Comic (via GMAO), p. 98

Translator's notes such as the above example have the pedagogical purpose of bringing the reader closer to what the translator perceives during the translation process when dealing with the ST. Doing so allows for deeper contextual understanding, as well as comprehension of foreignising techniques utilised by the translator.

The third article featured in *Manga Kenkanryū* by freelance journalist Takahiro Ōtsuki (pp. 234–239), is written largely in *da-tai* as the article by Nishimura. Ōtsuki's article, however, is much more emotive, with some sentences ending bluntly with nouns and grammar normally reserved for speech giving the writing a blunt feel:

ST: 何より、普通の人はいちいちそんなことばかり考えて暮らしてないし。

TT: And, above all, normal people just don't spend their days thinking about such things.

Source: (Japanese ST) *Manga Kenkanryū*, (English TT) *Hate Hallyu: The Comic*, p. 234

In the previous example, the negated form of *kurashite-iru* (Jp. 暮らしている), *kurashite-inai* (Jp. 暮らしていない), is conjugated as *kurashite-nai* (Jp. 暮らしてない) ending with the conjunction *shi* (Jp. し). The usage of both items is casual compared to what may be seen in *dearu-tai*. In the TT this difference has been signified using a conjugation in *don't spend their days* (versus *do not spend their days*) and at the beginning of the sentence, the latter less common in formal English academic writing, not unlike the use of the conjunction *shi* at the end of the ST sentence.

Language on the sentence and paragraph levels also differs from the first two articles, with a large proportion of long sentences. These features have been reproduced in the TT but in a restrained manner, so as to retain an adequate level of readability, as the Japanese language generally allows for much longer sentences than English:

ST: 先日の反日暴動、靖国参拝問題での執拗なからみ方、何より身の回りを見渡してもそういう「アジア」系外国人による犯罪ってやつも増えているみたいだし、なんか知らないけどあいつらってうざくね？ーそういう "気分" は間違いなく、われわれニッポン人の間に高まってきている。

TT: Anti-Japanese riots, the way they persistently pester about the prime-minister's visits to Yasukuni shrine, and growing crimes by 'Asian' foreigners wherever you look; these are all undoubtedly things that are increasing "feelings" within us Japanese like "I don't know why, but aren't those guys a nuisance?".

Source: (Japanese ST) *Manga Kenkanryū*, (English TT) *Hate Hallyu: The Comic*, p. 234

The previous segment could be split into two or even three in English, but this would take away from the feel of ST tone, where Ōtsuki is making a seemingly emotional, long-winded address to the readers of *Manga Kenkanryū*. The sentence used in this example would also contain a translator's note to bring attention to an important orthographic element in the ST. When Ōtsuki states "us Japanese" (Jp. われ われニッポン人, *ware-ware nippon-jin*) he chooses to do so using an emotive variant for the word 'Japan' (*nippon*, versus *nihon*) (*TV Asahi Nihongo Kyōshitsu*, 2017). In addition to using the more emotive variant, Ōtsuki also makes the choice of using *katakana* script, versus the standard *kanji*, or *hiragana* options. The Japanese writing system consists of four main scripts; *hiragana*, *katakana*, *kanji*, and *romaji*. Use of the various scripts sometimes serves the function of conveying various nuances and connotations based on their individual visual appearance (cf. Kess & Miyamoto, 1999; Hiraga, 2006), as well as representing sociolinguistic aspects such as non-fluency and foreignness (Robertson, 2016). Ōtsuki's use of *katakana* coupled with the emotive/patriotic variant of *Japan* (which may be compared to referring to, for example, Australians and New Zealanders as *Aussies* and *Kiwis*, respectively) gives emphasis that is difficult to reproduce in English. As there were no options other than simply *Japanese* (*Jap*, the only existing variant for *Japanese* in English, carries very negative connotations), I deemed supplementation with the following translator's note the most appropriate choice:

> **TN**: The author writes 'Japanese' using '*nippon-jin*' (Jp. ニッポン人) instead of the more standard '*nihon-jin*' (Jp. 日本人) in *katakana* script (what would more commonly be *kanji*). This may be seen as an emotive choice and a form of emphasis, not unlike the use of 'Aussie' or 'Kiwi' when Australians and New Zealanders refer to themselves, respectively (*TV Asahi Nihongo Kyōshitsu*, 2017).
>
> *Source: Hate Hallyu: The Comic* (via *GMAO*), p. 234

The final article, by Takushoku University professor Masao Shimojō, is written using yet another convention, with the writer opting to use *masu-tai* (Jp. ます体). The key feature of *masu-tai* is, as its name states, the formal verb ending *masu*. Here it should be noted that "formal" does not necessarily mean that *dearu-tai* and *da-tai* are informal. The usage of the three forms is largely an issue pertaining to style, with *masu* being used more commonly in formal spoken Japanese and written communication. In the case of Shimojō's usage, the article is written in a spoken style, as though the writer was addressing the readers directly. This interaction between writer and reader is made evident with Shimojō's closing sentence:

ST: 皆さんも一緒に日韓の将来を考えてください。
　　TT: I hope that you, too, join in and think about the future of Japan and South Korea.

Source: (Japanese ST) *Manga Kenkanryū*, (English TT) *Hate Hallyu: The Comic*, p. 267

In the previous example, Shimojō is asking readers to join in thinking about Japan-South Korea relations. This is clearer in the ST, as the readers are addressed directly using *mina-san* (Jp. 皆さん), which is a polite way of saying *everyone* but less awkward/archaic than *ladies and gentlemen*, thus a choice was made to include *I hope you, too* at the beginning of the sentence.

Translating image

Image, arguably the key feature of the comic, is a challenging aspect of translation. The task of multi-modal translation may involve the translation of pure image form, such as illustrations, as well as other para-textual elements including onomatopoeias and orthographic elements such as different script types. There has been increasing research on multi-modal translation (cf. Chapter 3), something that may be seen as a result of growth and development in the field of translation studies and rise in global popularity of the comic format.

Translating a visual text that is also of a controversial, political nature, such as *Manga Kenkanryū*, involves further challenges including ethical and technical issues. The methodology employed in this project proposes the application of the software GMAO in the translation of such documents, particularly in a setting with a pedagogical purpose. The use of GMAO allows for effective resolution of a number of ethical and technological issues.

One of the most beneficial features of GMAO is the ability to address multi-modal elements without the need to modify the original image, which is often a legal issue as translators of official/publishable translations are required to seek author permission to modify images in the ST. Modifying images can also pose technological problems. In the case of Japanese-English *manga* translation, layout of TT content has to be carefully thought out due to space restrictions. Space restrictions are usually a result of the difference in Japanese and English writing conventions, with Japanese predominantly written from top to bottom, right to left. Japanese also utilises a large number of Sino-Japanese compounds, which tend to highly compact vocabulary. As a result, a two-character compound (written together) can translate to two or three words in English. This expansion means that in order to fit the speech bubbles, font has to be down-sized or translations have to be modified so as to fit. Manipulating font size has limitations (e.g., potentially lower readability), whilst shortening sentences can result in incomplete inter-lingual transfer. As GMAO allows for the TT to go alongside (over) the ST, issues such as those aforementioned may be avoided, at the same time also providing the target readership with immediate access to the ST for comparative purposes.

Manga Kenkanryū has been widely criticised for its satirical depiction of characters, particularly those from a Korean ethnic background (cf., e.g., Goman, 2007; Sakamoto & Allen, 2007; Liscutin, 2009), Yamano adding a disclaimer in later editions and volumes from the series, stating that: "whilst drawing so as to exaggerate certain character features may be pointed out as being discrimination, it is an important method of expression in *manga*" (Yamano, 2015). This exaggeration is something that is not directly discussed in the translation here, bar the mention made by the author in the official disclaimer. The author's choice to depict characters in such a manner is contextually self-explanatory, and commenting on the issue would go against the project purpose of creating an unbiased resource.

As discussed earlier, one of the great advantages of using software such as GMAO in multi-modal translation is the ability to present a TT that is layered over the ST, thus giving readers the power to access both readily. As aforementioned, this two-dimensional form is particularly beneficial when the translation purpose is pedagogical, as the readership are given access not only to the ST and TT but also, through the availability of extended translator's notes, the translation process itself.

The value of the ability to superimpose translation over image is most evident when dealing with complex, culture-bound paratextual elements such as visual metaphor. The translation of metaphors and idioms is one of the most challenging tasks faced by translators. As discussed in earlier chapters, the methodologies for metaphor translation are relevant to both literary and non-literary translation and have been extensively discussed in translation studies, notably by Broeck (1978), Newmark (1981), Toury (1995), and, in more recent times, Schäffner (2012). Visual metaphors often carry no textual cues and can be found in other visual media such as cartoons and film. Although the first volume of *Manga Kenkanryū* does not contain any visual metaphors, they are prevalent in the later volumes (2–5). As the translation of visual metaphors is of relevance to the text type (graphic novel), it is worthwhile to include a couple of examples of visual metaphor from other volumes so as to illustrate the full function of the proposed methodology.

In volume two of *Manga Kenkanryū* (2006), in the final chapter (titled 'epilogue', as is the case with the last chapter of *Manga Kenkanryū 1*) Yamano, the author, makes an appearance to discuss media and public response since the publication of the first volume. As part of this discussion, Yamano mentions that there are two comics being written by South Korean authors in response to *Manga Kenkanryū*, titled *Manga Ken'nichiryū* ('Hate Japanese Wave' – Jp. マンガ嫌日流, Kr. 만화 혐일류, *Manhwa Hyeomillyu*).[4] After citing a South Korean news source as to the quality of one of the publications, three of the main characters in *Manga Kenkanryū* make the following statement:

ST: 金城摸氏、胸をワクワクさせながら首を長くしてお待ちしております！

TT: Mr. Seong-Mo Kim, we extend our necks with hearts beating in excitement and anticipation!

Source: Manga Kenkanryū 2 and English translation, p. 269 (Yamano, 2006; translation mine)

The comment is part of the following images, showing the three protagonists with elongated necks and beating hearts:

Figure 6.1 Manga Kenkanryū 2, p. 269 (Yamano, 2006)

Although the translation, which is quite literal, does make some sense *descriptively*, the metaphorical meaning contained within the ST is lost. Utilising GMAO, the image would be supplemented with a translator's note such as the following:

TN: "To extend one's neck" (Jp. 首を長くして待つ, *kubi wo nagaku shite matsu*) is a Japanese metaphor meaning "to await eagerly/ eagerly look forward to". It is a variation of the metaphor "await with a crane's neck" (Jp. 鶴首して待つ, *kakushu-shite matsu*).

Source: example of translator's note via GMAO

The reader is, thus, able to immediately access an important translator's note that aids in otherwise hindered contextual comprehension. The exaggerated image of characters with extended necks and beating hearts, an important paratextual element, is not completely clarified by the translation of the accompanying text itself. It is such instances that require delving into multi-modal translation which, as discussed in earlier sections of this chapter, can pose problems without the use of technology such as GMAO.

A further example of how GMAO may be used in multi-modal translation relates to onomatopoeia and mimesis, a much more common issue within graphic novel translation. Onomatopoeia and mimesis, which are used to express sounds and certain states (such as even the 'state of silence'), are a common feature of *manga* (Fukuda, 1993; Inose, 2008). Japanese *manga* make extensive use of onomatopoeia (Jp. 擬音語・擬声語, *giongo/giseigo*) and mimesis (Jp. 擬態語, *gitaigo*). A distinct feature of Japanese onomatopoeia and mimesis is their highly visual presentation within the medium, with relevant terms displayed using highly decorative fonts of varying sizes. Onomatopoeia and mimesis are not just words – they come in many varieties of shapes and sizes, helping to add emphasis to the context. *Manga Kenkanryū*, although highly political in nature, is no exception, with numerous examples of both onomatopoeia and mimesis. It should be noted here that onomatopoeia and mimesis, although seemingly more simple than visual metaphors, often pose greater technological issues. One of the main problems when translating these paratextual elements is editing. Text may be incorporated into the surrounding image, even partially covered by it. The most visually pleasing method of dealing with the issue is to edit the image using software such as *Photoshop*: this process involves erasing the original onomatopoeia/mimesis and replacing it with the translation in a similar looking font. The task also usually involves skewing and twisting text so as to achieve the same effect as

in the ST, a process so complex and time-consuming that it is seldom prac-
tised in *manga* translation. Thus, as with other aforementioned multi-modal
elements, the use of GMAO greatly aided in the translation process, allowing
for very simple overlaying of TT. The following effect was achieved:

Figure 6.2 Manga Kenkanryū and example of GMAO translation, p. 97

As GMAO also allows for extended translator's notes, it is also possible to provide readers with additional information relating to more complex cases of onomatopoeia and mimesis. In English, some sounds are rarely reproduced into text, thus meaning that the English rendering is whatever the translator thinks is appropriate. The outcome is not always target readership comprehension – the sound energetic running in Japanese, for example, is *do-do-do* (Jp. ド ド ド). This may be translated into English as, for example, *dm-dm-dm* or *tap-tap-tap* or any other sound the translator may choose. Unless accompanied by relevant imagery in close proximity to the text, such a translation may not necessarily make sense to the target readership, thus resulting in reduced comprehension. An example of the extent of onomatopoeias and mimesis used in Japanese *manga* may be seen on page 9 of *Manga Kenkanryū*:

Figure 6.3 Manga Kenkanryū, p. 9

This particular page has a total of six onomatopoeia and mimesis (out of a total of 7 *koma* – cells). These include *zu-za-za-za-za* (sound of energetic lunge/slide – Jp. ズザザザザ), *hyoi* (sound/state of suddenly/unexpected movement – Jp. ひょい), *do-kama* (sound of strong kick – Jp. ドカマッ), *ba-sa* (sound of a net – Jp. バサッ), and *gakkuri* (state of falling/lowering one's head in disappointment – Jp. がっくり). Readers well acquainted with English translations of Japanese *manga* may have the ability to 'feel' what a translation such as *dm-dm-dm* or even Romanisation of the ST term *do-do-do* contextually means; however, this cannot be guaranteed. In an earlier translation of the first chapter of *Manga Kenkanryū* (2012), a different approach was taken to translating onomatopoeia and mimesis:

Figure 6.4 Hate Hallyu: The Comic, p. 9

The approach involved the translation method mentioned earlier in this section – replacement of onomatopoeia and mimesis utilising *Photoshop* editing. Although an approach that is to some more aesthetically pleasing (indeed, there is a *manga* readership that is strongly against any kind visual of manipulation of the ST), the approach is not as educational as the one utilising GMAO. Through the use of GMAO, the translator is able to create a TT alongside the ST with ample space for translator's notes, thus resulting in increased, conscious reader recognition of the ST.

TN 1: *Swoosh*, (Jp. *Zu-za-za-za-za*, ズザザザザ) is an onomatopoeia used to describe the sound of a sliding movement. In this case, Kan-ame is attempting a slide-tackle.

TN 2: *Thump*, (Jp. *Do-kama*, ドカマツ) is an onomatopoeia used to describe the sound of a powerful strike. In this case, Takao has struck a football with force.

TN 3: *Slide*, (Jp. *Zu-za-za-za-za-za*, ズザザザザザ) see TN1, same page. The context shows Kaname failing in his slide-tackle, sliding off into the distance. The source text 'zu-za-za-za-za' is in a more jagged layout so as to illustrate failure for increased comical effect. A choice was made to use 'slide' here as opposed to 'swoosh', so as to express the state of Kaname's failure.

TN 4: *Poing*, (Jp. *Hyoi*, ひょい) is mimesis used to describe a state of sudden and unexpected movement. In this case, Takao has quickly evaded Kaname's slide-tackle, flicking the football behind him.

TN 5: *Swissh*, (Jp. *Ba-sa*, バサツ) is an onomatopoeia used to describe the sound of a light surface such as a net being hit by some-thing. In this instance, a football has hit the back of a goal.

TN 6: *Humpf*, (Jp. *Gakkuri*, がっくり) is mimesis used to describe a state of disappointment, often resulting in the lowering of one's head. In this case, Kaname is disappointed in having lost a goal to Takao in spite of his efforts with the slide-tackle. *Gakkuri* is written in *hiragana*, using thick, heavy-looking font.

Source: example of translator's note via GMAO

This is not to say that the previous translation example is inferior: judge-ment of quality largely depends on the project purpose. The previous exam-ple would thus be better suited for popular consumption, where aesthetics is more important. In a pedagogical approach such as that chosen for the project at hand, translator input, in other words, the translation process itself, carries much greater importance, as it allows readers to assess the TT as a source and/or resource for further research.

Thus, as proposed in this new methodology, an approach utilising GMAO contains the same translations for onomatopoeia and mimesis as in other approaches but is not inserted as a replacement of the ST image; rather it is superimposed in a second layer, together with colour coded translator's notes. In the case of the previous example, the following translator's notes would be included (see above).

GMAO thus allows for extended translator's notes that may be used to discuss terminology in greater detail. Care was (and ought to be) taken so as not to include information that is less relevant to general comprehension, such as further usage examples and etymology. It should be noted, however, that the utilisation of a platform such as GMAO may indeed allow for more linguistically focused translator's notes, if that is the purpose of the translation (e.g., linguistic study of onomatopoeia/mimesis in *manga*).

Lexicon-Specific Analysis

Whereas the first section of this chapter discussed more general issues confronted during the translation process, this section focuses on specific word-choice related issues divided by chapter. Volume one of *Manga Kenkanryū* is divided into nine chapters plus an epilogue and special, as well as four articles by authors other than Yamano (discussed earlier). As *Manga Kenkanryū* is largely concerned with Japan-Korea relations, a large proportion of the lexicon discussed in the following sections is of political and/or historical nature. Not all of the nine chapters will be discussed, however, as although translation choices made based on the methodology were carried out throughout the complete translation process, there was repetition of certain terminology (such as, for example, the many ways of referring to *Korea* discussed in section 1).

The general approach taken throughout translation was to evaluate terms in a 'neutral' manner based on my own knowledge and experience. As discussed in earlier chapters, in reality what constitutes 'neutral' is highly subjective and debatable, hence the approach utilising GMAO, which allows for greater clarity and evaluation of the translation process by the target readership and other third-parties. 'Neutrality' may thus be seen as an ideal, GMAO playing the function of a tool used to illustrate this concept.

Chapter 1: Japan-South Korea World Cup

Chapter 1 of *Manga Kenkanryū* (translated as *Hate Hallyu: The Comic*) discusses issues pertaining to the Japan-South Korea Football World Cup as well as serving a more general function of introducing to the readers the protagonist Okiayu Kaname and some of his friends. The chapter contains a large amount of onomatopoeia and mimesis, particularly in the first half of the chapter where their function is to help illustrate movement.

Issues faced during the translation of Chapter 1 include transliteration of South Korean football player names, some of which appear to have been misspelled in the Japanese ST. As discussed in the previous section, proper names were translated using the most popularly available English transliteration. In the case of athlete names, sources such as the official Fédération Internationale de Football Association (FIFA) and Korean Football Association (KFA) were used as reference. In case of ambiguities, further contextual analysis was made. On page 17, for example, there is mention of Choe Jin-Il carrying out a follow-through right-left lariat attack on Tommasi. South Korea's 2002 World Cup squad, however, did not contain any players by the name *Jin-Il*. Further contextual research found that the South Korean player involved in the incident was Choi Jin-Chul. Here it should be noted that, although the project methodology dictated a choice not to correct serious ST mistakes/inaccuracies, this choice only pertains to correcting historical and/or subjective errors. The name of the player in question is a factual error, and based on surrounding contextual accuracy (i.e., incident involving Tommasi and accuracy of other listed athlete names and events) it was not something that was done intentionally by the author. The choice, thus, was made to list the incorrect spelling accompanied by translation note with a suggestion of the correct transliteration.

Other issues in Chapter 1 included the translation of perhaps some of the most important proper nouns in the publication – *Kankoku, Kita-Chōsen*, and *Chōsen* (all of which denote *Korea*), translation of which has been discussed in section 1 of this chapter. An interesting issue faced early on in the project that has been supplemented by translator's notes pertains to the very title of the publication. An issue that has been briefly discussed in an earlier publication (Zulawnik, 2016), the title of the *Manga Kankanryū* series used on the cover of the publication divides lexical items using different font, effectively altering the intended contextual framing of the discourse:

Figure 6.5 Cover of *Manga Kenkanryū* (Yamano, 2005)

As seen in the previous example, Yamano has included a small text box in the left-hand corner of the cover that states *manga*, followed by *Ken-Kan-Ryu* in *romaji*. Below that is the character '*Ken*' in a red, coarse-looking font, followed by *Kanryū* in a blue, standard font. The red and blue colour scheme is most likely representative of the colours of the yin-yang symbol of the South Korean flag, whilst the difference in font between *Ken* and *Kanryū* is used to put emphasis on the idea of hate aimed towards the Hallyu phenomenon (cf. Chapters 1 and 2) as opposed to, for example, Korea or the Korean race in general.

This distinction is difficult to make phonetically, as *kenkan* (Jp. 嫌韓, literally *Hate South Korea*), a term broadly used to refer to general distaste of Korea is written using the same characters, with *ryū* commonly used as a suffix meaning *style*, *wave*, or *tendency*. Thus, without the emphasis provided on the cover, the title could be interpreted not as *Ken-kanryū* (Jp. 嫌韓流, i.e., *Hate [the] Korean Wave*) but as *Kenkan-ryu* (Jp. 嫌韓流, i.e., *Hate-Korea Wave*).

As to whether or not the publication is ultimately enticing, the latter is something that must be decided by the reader, based on the discourse and tone, as well as the author's own remarks defending the 'movement' as in fact being the former (in other words, a 'movement' against the Korean wave of popular culture through understanding of Japan-Korea relations). The fact that such a decision has to be made by readers places even greater importance on the translation, as the purpose is not to try to lead readership to either conclusion – it is to lead the readership to further inquiry.

The final section of Chapter 1 is part of a six-piece mini-topic series about additional issues not discussed within the chapters titled *Far East Asia Investigation Committee Report*. *File 01* on pages 35–36 is a discussion about *fire disease* (Kr. 화병, *hwappyeong*, Japanised as *fabyon*, 火病), reportedly a psychological disorder "exclusive to the Korean people". The issue with translating this section was, once again, a choice between using an English glossed-translation based on the Chinese characters (as previously: *fire disease*) or transliteration. In case of the latter, a choice would then have to be made as to whether use the Japanese or Korean pronunciation for the term. The ST lists the Chinese characters (*fire* and *disease*) as well as the Japanese transliteration for the Korean name. Contextually, the characters in the ST are using Japanese to talk about a Korean term; however the most commonly used term in English is the transliterated Korean *hwappyeong*. As the ST also lists the Chinese characters (which all Japanese speakers can immediately understand as meaning *fire disease*), the following translator's note is included:

TN: 'Fire Disease' (Jp. fabyon, Kr. hwappyeong 火病) is a glossed translation based on the meaning of the Chinese characters. 'Fabyon' is the Japanese rendition of the Korean pronunciation, whilst 'hwappyeong' is the revised Korean Romanisation.

Source: example of translator's note via GMAO, p. 35

The translator's note is brief, only listing basic information necessary for understanding similar to that available to the ST readership. It does not specifically engage with the ST discourse or the author's opinions. As with earlier examples, readers ar`e also provided with relevant transcriptions in both Japanese and Korean allowing for further inquiry. Here it should be noted that the ST also lists *hwa-pyung* as an English spelling of the word; however, as this is currently a non-standard Romanisation method for Korean (and is already included in the ST) it has been omitted from the translator's note.

Chapter 2: Post-war Compensation Problem

Chapter 2 of *Manga Kenkanryū* broadly discusses the issue of post-war compensations, with *Far East Asia Investigation Committee Report File 02* providing a brief talk about South Korean international aid work seen during the 2004 Indian Ocean earthquake and tsunami. In the chapter, the protagonist, Kaname, and his girlfriend, Itsumi, take part in a debate titled the 'Japan-South Korea Compensation Problem'. The chapter contains a number of key terms commonly come across when dealing with Japan-Korea relations in the Japanese and Korean languages.

When discussing the issue of compensation in Japan-Korea relations the first term requiring close analysis is just that – *compensation*. There has been a lot of discussion about the importance of language in politics including translation in political discourse (cf. e.g., Sharifian, 2009; Tymoczko, 2014; Chomsky, 2015); Japan-Korea relations and the issue of *compensation* is no exception (Park, 2000, 2013/2014).

Chapter 2 of *Manga Kenkanryū*, titled 'Post-War Compensation Problem: Eternally sought-after money and abject apologies' contains the general umbrella term *hoshō* (Jp. 補償) which may be translated as *reparation*, *compensation*, and *indemnity*. *Hoshō* is a Sino-Japanese compound also used with the same meaning in the Chinese and Korean languages. The compound is made up of two characters denoting *to compensate*; *supplement*; *make up for* (Jp. *oginau*, 補う) and *atone for*; *compensate*; *pay back* (Jp. *tsugunau*, 償う). A term that is often used alongside (or in place of) *hoshō* is *baishō* (Jp. 賠償) which, whilst also a Sino-Japanese compound commonly used in the Chinese and Korean languages, consists of characters both denoting *atone for*; *compensate*; *pay back* (the second character, *shō*, is the same in both compounds). Both terms are used in the chapter, thus making a distinction is crucial, particularly as the usage is often a source of debate on whether or not the Japanese government efforts thus far have been sufficient and/or appropriate. Whereas *hoshō* is more commonly used with *sengo* (post-war) to mean *post-war compensation*, *baishō* is often paired with *sensō* (war) to mean *war reparations* or *kokka* (nation) to mean *state indemnity* (*Randomhouse*, 1994; *Kenkyusha*, 2008; *Genius*, 2008). The terms, however, are not always used with accuracy, in spite of carrying a different meaning, sometimes leading to confusion and controversy. Official Japanese documents pertaining to post-war compensation additionally utilise the native Japanese term *tsugunai* (Jp. 償い), which also carries a nuance of *atonement* and *apology*. This nuanced term has no equivalent in the Korean language, something that Park (2013/2014), discusses with reference to the comfort women issue and Wada's own research into the topic:

> The (Asian Women's) fund was considered a 'civil' entity, however in reality it was an arrangement where "in case fundraising from the public is insufficient, government capital shall be used for supplementation, thus meaning that ultimately atonement is financed with contributions from the nation as well as government capital" (Wada, 2012, p. 63). Professor Wada has the following to say regarding the details of how the fund's compensation money came to be known as 'atonement money': "'Atonement', the term used by the fund, was used differently to 'compensation'. In English, *hoshō* and *tsugunai* were translated as 'compensation' and 'atonement', respectively. *Atonement* is a religious term in English, meaning *redemption* or *atonement for sin*. Writing atonement with a capital letter preceded by *the* results in *the Atonement*, which refers to Jesus' Redemption. Based on this distinction, the fund's undertaking was to convey that they were functioning based on apology. This may be related as to why the Philippines and Netherlands, which received explanation in English from the fund, had comparatively more understanding about the project. In the Korean language, it is not possible to differentiate *hoshō* and *tsugunai*, both terms ending up as '보상' (*bosang*).
>
> (Park, 2013/2014, pp. 270–271, my translation)

It is thus clear that great care must be taken when translating terms such as *hoshō*, *baishō*, and *tsugunai*. As aforementioned, in the project at hand, special care was taken to make a distinction between the two most commonly used terms, with the addition of a translator's note with the ST terms:

TN: '*Compensation*' refers to the Japanese word *hoshō* (補償).
TN: '*reparation*' refers to the Japanese word *baishō* (賠償).

Source: example of translator's note via GMAO, p. 45 & p. 51

Two other terms requiring special consideration in Chapter 2 relate to the issue of Japanese sincerity in expression of regret for invasion during World War Two and the events it entailed. The first term, *hansei* (Jp. 反省), which appears throughout *Manga Kenkanryū*, when in noun form may be translated as *reflection, introspection, soul-searching*, and *reconsideration* (*Kenkyūsha*, 2008). As a verb, *hansei-suru* may be colloquially translated simply as *think about* as in *think about what you've done! Hansei* is related in meaning to *kōkai* (*regret*), reflective of the *soul-searching* translation variant mentioned earlier. In *Manga Kenkanryū* the term is often used by characters portrayed as 'anti-Japanese' or 'left-wing' in their interpretations of Japan's wartime past.

Although *hansei* may be generally translated without issue as *reflection* when in noun form, situations where it is used as a verb or adjective pose contextual problems:

ST: アジアの方々との友好と平和を希求する私達の立場から見ると日本は過去の行いについて全く反省していないと言わざるを得ません。

 TT: From our viewpoint of those seeking friendship and peace with the people of Asia, it must be said that Japan is completely unreflective of its past actions.

Source: (Japanese ST) *Manga Kenkanryū*, (English TT – draft) *HH: The Comic*, p. 45

The previous text box is an example of usage of the verb form of *hansei*. A member of the debate panel opposing the protagonist Kaname and his girlfriend Itsumi makes an opening statement about Japan's alleged lack of reflection in regard to the 'past'. The negative continuous form of the verb *hansei-suru, hansei-shite-inai*, sounds unnatural when translated as *unreflective* in English. Natural sounding alternatives that come to mind are, for example, *oblivious, impervious, unconcerned*, and *indifferent*.

The problem with using such an alternative, however, is its detachment from the ST nuance of 'reflection'. In fact, further deconstructive examination of the term *hansei* reveals that it also manifests complex semantic properties as it is used as a translation of the archaic English term *reflexion* used in philosophy as in *self-reflection* and *introspection* (*Kōjien*, 2008). It would therefore be beneficial to retain *reflection* as a translation of *hansei* albeit through the modification of the TT sentence structure:

TT (EX1): From our viewpoint of those seeking friendship and peace with the people of Asia, it must be said that Japan is completely unreflective of its past actions.

TT (EX2): From our viewpoint of those seeking friendship and peace with the people of Asia, it must be said that Japan completely lacks reflection when it comes to its past actions.

Source: (English TT – Draft and final) *HH: The Comic*, p. 45

The rephrased translation allows for the retention of the key term *reflection* whilst also sounding natural. This alternative grammatical structure also allows for the use of 'when it comes to' which is closer to the ST in that it utilises the semantically equivalent *ni-tsuite* (Jp. について). A translator's note is not required for *hansei* as the semantic qualities of the term have been effectively preserved in the TT.

A further term that required particular analysis during translation of Chapter 2 was *seisan* (Jp. 清算), which may be translated as *payment*, *clearance*, or *liquidation*, but in historical and political contexts generally means *come to terms with* (the past/history), *close the books* (on a dispute), or *put the past behind* (*Kenkyūsha*, 2008). As with many of the examples in this chapter, the exact same Sino-compound is also used in the Korean language (Kr. *cheongsan*, 청산). In spite of various widely available dictionary translations (e.g., *Kenkyūsha*, 2008; *Weblio*, 2017; *Dong-A*, 2005), the term, in reality, embodies much more complex, contextually varying semantic values, which pose issues during translation, one such example in Figure 6.6:

The photo, taken from the *Korean Central News Agency* (*KCNA*)'s website, shows a group of delegates at what is titled in English the Asian Regional Symposium Demanding Liquidation of Japan's Past. This is a rather literal translation of the Korean title *Ilbon wi gwageo cheongsam eul yogu haneun asia jiyeok toronhoe* (Kr. 일본의 과거청산을 요구하는 아시아지역토론회) which, for ease of comparison, may be directly translated into Japanese as *Nihon no kako seisan wo yōkyū-suru ajia chi'iki tōronkai* (Jp. 日本の過去清算を要求するアジア地域討論会). Whilst the title makes perfect sense in Korean and Japanese, two translation issues that immediately come to mind when considering the English are *demanding* (where the Korean *yogu* and Japanese *yōkyū* more appropriately translate as *seeking*), and the subject of this section, *liquidation of Japan's past*.

Figure 6.6 Example of translation for *cheongsan* (*Korean Central News Agency*, 2002)

The previous example of a less than perfect translation is particularly useful as, like in the previous example, *seisan* often happens to be coupled with *kako*, meaning *past* (as in *past, present, future*). Such usage is also the case in *Manga Kenkanryū*, with further examples in Chapter 8. In Chapter 2, *seisan* appears just one frame after the aforementioned *hansei* (*reflection*) example:

ST: 戦前戦中、朝鮮の方々に与えた有形無形の被害の清算が全くなされていないのは事実であり、私達、良心的日本人としては日本政府に責任を取らせなくてはならないと考えています。

TT: It is a fact that atonement for material and immaterial damage that was done to the people of Joseon before and during the war has not been realised at all, and I think that as good-hearted Japanese, we must make the government of Japan take responsibility.

Source: (Japanese ST) *Manga Kenkanryū*, (English TT) *HH: The Comic*, p. 45

In the previous example, *seisan* has been translated as *atone*. Whilst *resolve* may be just as appropriate, the term has a direct equivalent in Japanese in the form of *kaiketsu* (Jp. 解決), which features two pages later (p. 47). As with earlier examples, special care has been taken so as to ensure both contextual equivalence and consistency. *Atone* is defined as: "make amends or reparation. Middle English (originally in the sense 'make or become united or reconciled' . . .): from *at one* in early use; later by back-formation from atonement" (*Oxford*, 2005), with *atonement* further defined as "[mass noun] the action of making amends for a wrong or injury" (*Oxford*, 2005).

Atone has been mentioned earlier in this chapter with reference to *hoshō* and *tsugunai*, however it should be noted that the term is not used in the TT in reference to other terminology as *tsugunai* does not feature in the publication. It is an appropriate translation choice for *seisan* as one may argue that the "resolution of the past" that many are seeking from Japan is the making of amends for 'wrong or injury', which is further contextually justified by the usage exemplified earlier ('material and immaterial damage').

As further supplementation for the previous translation, a translator's note has been included to highlight linguistic features of the ST that were deemed best left untranslated as this would require a high level of domestication, potentially leading to hyper-translation:

TN: In the ST, this character uses what may be deemed as Japanese too formal for the situation (a debate where supposedly neutral facts are being exchanged), using '*Chōsen no kata-gata*', an honorific plural form of '*Chōsen no hito-bito*'/*Chōsen-jin*' meaning 'the Joseon people'. Such usage generally implies greater empathy for the subject in question and may also relate to character building based on the fact the character is portrayed as a 'pro-citizen' (Jp. *puro-shimin*, プロ市民) (see note from author on same page for definition).

Source: example of translator's note via GMAO

The final issue requiring discussion in Chapter 2 is *puro-shimin* (noted in the previous translator's note), which the characters taking part in the debate are labelled as by the protagonist:

ST: 百戦錬磨のプロ市民が相手という、圧倒的に不利な状況
   TT: An overwhelmingly unfavourable situation with battle hardened pro-citizens* as opponents.

Source: (Japanese ST) *Manga Kenkanryū*, (English TT) *HH: The Comic*, p. 46

As *puro-shimin* is a relatively recent addition to the standard Japanese lexicon and is in fact referenced with a side-note from the author with a definition, the choice was made to make a literal translation in the form of *pro-citizen*. A translation of the note created by the author defining the term is sufficient for understanding:

ST: ＊プロ市民．．．．．．．職業的(プロフェッショナル)市民運動家の略。一般市民を装い、市民活動と称して政治的、営利的な活動を行う人や団体を揶揄した言い方。活動領域は、平和、護憲、人権、反核、アジアへの謝罪、環境保護など多岐に渡っている。

TT: ＊ Pro-Citizen. . . . . . Abbreviation for professional (pro) citizen activist. A satirical term used to refer to people or organisations who carry out political and for-profit activities in the name of civilian activity under the pretence of being regular civilians. Areas of activity range widely with topics like peace, protection of the Constitution, human rights, the anti-nuclear movement, apology to Asia, and environmental protection.

Source: (Japanese ST) *Manga Kenkanryū*, (English TT) *HH: The Comic*, p. 46

The ST uses the term *shokugyōteki* (Jp. 職業的), which is a literal Japanese translation of *professional* (also commonly used in Japanese as a loanword). As the Sino-Japanese compound, *shokugyōteki* is more formal than the loanword *purofeshonaru* (Jp. プロフェッショナル), the effect of which has been replicated in the TT through '*professional (pro)*', where '*professional*' (the more formal term) is followed by '*pro*'.

Chapter 3: Origins of the Zainichi *South Koreans and Joseon Koreans*

Chapter 3 of *Manga Kenkanryū* discusses the historical origins of Korean permanent residents in Japan, also known as *zainichi kankokujin* (Jp. 在日韓国人, used to refer to Koreans of South Korean origin or those who identify with South Korea), *zainichi chōsenjin* (Jp. 在日朝鮮人, used for Koreans of North Korean origin or those who identify with North Korea) or just *zainichi* for short (Jp. 在日, general term, often seen as derogatory). Chapter 3 is one of the shortest in the publication and comes in the form of a history lesson-like discussion between Kaname, his girlfriend

Itsumi, and their university senior Ryūhei Sueyuki. The chapter is concluded by the article by Kanji Nishio discussed in the first section of this chapter.

The first term requiring discussion is *zainichi*, which features for the first time in Chapter 1. Although in the translation the term is first defined in Chapter 1, the concept of *zainichi* Koreans is not discussed in much detail before Chapter 3, where it is the main topic. There are various ways in which the term *zainichi* has been translated according to context. *Zainichi* as a word does not indicate any specific ethnic denomination as it simply means (living) *in Japan*. Technically, it is a short-form of *zainichi gaikoku-jin* meaning *foreigner(s) residing in Japan*, a large proportion of whom historically happen to be Korean (*Japan Times*, 2016). This statistical presence has led to the term *zainichi* becoming almost exclusively synonymous with Koreans living in Japan. As mentioned earlier, on its own, *zainichi* also carries a lot of stigma as it is seldom used in official settings. Neither is it a completely negative term – prominent ethnic Korean personalities in Japan also use the term in, for example, self-reference.

In *Manga Kenkanryū* the term *zainichi* is used rather conservatively, usually accompanied by *kankoku-jin/chōsen-jin* (South Korean/Joseon Korean), presumably putting emphasis on the fact that ethnic Koreans in Japan usually identify with a certain faction based on cultural upbringing and personal political views.[5] In the translation this has been reflected through separate terms semantically and contextually equivalent to those used in the ST. As discussed earlier in the chapter, this involved retaining the Romanised *zainichi* followed by either *South Korean* or *Joseon Korean*, for *kankoku-jin* and *chōsen-jin*, respectively:

ST: まずは、日本に住んでいる在日韓国・朝鮮人のルーツから説明しようか

TT: First off, let's start by explaining the roots of the Zainichi South Koreans and Joseon Koreans living in Japan.

Source: (Japanese ST) *Manga Kenkanryū*, (English TT) *HH: The Comic*, p. 83

When *zainichi* is used on its own in the ST, the term is left Romanised in the TT, thus allowing for improved contextual comprehension and comparison. Doing so is important, as there are areas in the publication where one may argue a lack of consistency in usage. There are parts where characters emphasise that Koreans during the colonial period ('Joseon Koreans') were 'Japanese', later referring to the people of the period not as 'Japanese', but 'Joseon Korean'. Such inconsistencies are a feature of the ST that may be noticed through careful reading, and so in order for the TT to be able to function as an accurate representation of the original (in other words, something that may be used as a primary source) utmost care must be taken to retain consistency.

Perhaps the main issue discussed in chapter 3 which introduces yet another term requiring careful consideration is how '*zainichi* Koreans' came to live in Japan in the first place. The term that is most commonly used in the Japanese and Korean languages (and in the publication) is *kyōsei renkō* (Jp. 強制連行), where *kyōsei* means *force* or *forced* and *renkō* means *to move/bring* (someone somewhere). *Kyōsei renkō* is a term that is part of an ongoing, highly debated issue of volition (or lack of) when discussing Koreans (and other ethnic groups) that ended up in Japan from around the turn of the 20th century till the end of World War Two.

The term *kyōsei renkō* features as a subtitle for Chapter 3, signifying the term's importance. The problem with translating the term into English is the potential change in semantic value and impact. In Japanese and Korean, although made up of two compounds, the term is always written together as one word. Upon seeing the term, most Japanese and Korean readers will immediately think of the historical issues mentioned earlier. In translation, this is particularly an issue when the term is used as a means of movement followed by a verb as in the following instance:

> **ST**: だから強制連行でやって来た朝鮮人がいたとしても、みんな帰っていったはずなんだ。
>
> **TT**: That's why even if there were Joseon Koreans who came through forced movement, they should all have returned home.
>
> *Source:* (Japanese ST) *Manga Kenkanryū*, (English TT – draft) *HH: The Comic*, p. 85

In the previous example, *kyōsei renkō* is followed by *de yatte kita* meaning *came through/via*. Thus, there is semantic repetition in the sense that both *renkō* and *yatte kita* specify movement. In the ST this is not unnatural as *kyōsei renkō* is a complex compound that may be used as a mode of movement (i.e., forced movement). In English, however, it would be unnatural to say someone came/arrive via *forced movement*, as in the previous example. A further option for translation is:

ST: だから強制連行でやって来た朝鮮人がいたとしても、みんな帰っていったはずなんだ。
    TT: That's why even if there were Joseon Koreans who came by force, they should all have returned home.

Source: (Japanese ST) *Manga Kenkanryū*, (English TT – draft 2) *HH: The Comic*, p. 85

In the previous example, the ST *kyōsei renkō* and *yatte kita* have been simplified in the TT as *came by force*. Although the TT sounds natural, an important ST term (*kyōsei renkō*) has been omitted, creating problems with contextual comprehension and consistency. *Come by/be brought by force* does not carry the same semantic value as *forced movement*, which is a problem as *kyōsei renkō* does not change regardless of usage. Ultimately, the following choice was made:

TT: That's why even if there were Joseon Koreans who came through forced movement, they should all have returned home.
    TT: That's why even if there were Joseon Koreans who came by force, they should all have returned home.
    TT: That's why even if there were Joseon Koreans who were transported by force, they should all have returned home.

Source: (English TT – Draft 1, 2, and final) *HH: The Comic*, p. 85

By translating *kyōsei renkō* as *transportation by force* it is possible to use the term both as a proper noun and, when needed, modify *transportation* into a verb whilst still retaining *by force*. The term is additionally supplemented with the following translator's note early in the chapter:

> **TN**: 'Transportation by force' (Jp. *kyōsei renkō*, 強制連行) is written as one word in Japanese and Korean, always signifying the historical context discussed in this chapter.
>
> *Source:* example of translator's note via GMAO, p. 79

The note, thus, helps notify the TT reader that the TT term carries a certain form in the ST, which carries its own contextual significance. The information provided is intentionally unopinionated – a definition of *kyōsei renkō* beyond that given through the context by the ST author would contradict with the project methodology of creating an unbiased source. Readers of the TT would, of course, be made aware of the project methodology through the translation foreword and other framing tools (such as the use of GMAO).

Chapter 5: Threat of Anti-Japanese Mass Media

Following Chapter 4, which was about alleged South Korean appropriation of Japanese culture (and did not contain any particularly difficult to translate terms), Chapter 5 discusses the 'threat of anti-Japanese mass media'. Chapter 5 is also fairly standard, containing many important terms that have already been discussed in relation to other chapters (e.g., *Korea* and *zainichi*).

One issue that does require discussion, however, is the translation of the event known as '*chima-chogori kirisaki jiken*' (Jp. チマチョゴリ切り裂き事件). *Chima-chogori* is a transliteration of the Korean *chima jeogori* (Kr. 저고리), a traditional Korean dress made up of a skirt and short vest, whilst *kirisaki* is a noun form of the verb *kirisaku* meaning to *cut apart* or *cut up* (*jiken* simply means *event* or *case*). Most ST readers will be able to immediately identify the event upon reading the title because of pre-existing knowledge of Japanese current events. In the TT the event has been translated as the '*chima-jeogori cutting incident*' with the following translator's note:

> **TN**: 'Chima jeogori cutting incident' (Jp. chima chogori kirisaki jiken, チマ・チョゴリ切り裂き事件). The chima jeogori is a traditional Korean vest and skirt (Kr. chima jeogori, 치마저고리).
>
> *Source:* example of translator's note via GMAO, p. 146

As TT readers may not have pre-existing knowledge of the event, it is beneficial to include a brief translator's note with the ST term Romanised, as well as the original Japanese term allowing for further research and inquiry. Further development of a software such as *GMAO* may also allow for a copy-paste option, which would mean that TT readers could perform searches from, for example, the translator's notes. As the description of the details surrounding the event are quite detailed in the ST further explanation of the event in the translator's note was deemed unnecessary.

Chapter 6: Hangeul and the South Koreans

Chapter 6 of *Manga Kenkanryū* focuses on the Korean writing system (also known as the 'Korean alphabet'), *hangeul*. The protagonist, Kaname, is lectured by his university senior, Ryūhei, about alleged imperfections and downfalls of the writing system, including criticism regarding the choice to abolish Chinese characters (Kr. *hanja*, 한자). About halfway into the chapter, Ryūhei provides a Japanese example to show how *hangeul* is unsuited for homonyms in spite of there being so many Sino-Korean compounds in the Korean language. To do this, he lists five Sino-Japanese compounds that are homonyms (all pronounced *sōkan*) stating that "(Korean is) not only difficult to read, but it's also impossible to deal with homonyms" (*Manga Kenkanryū*, p. 166).

The great irony here is, however, the fact that the five Sino-Japanese compounds listed by Ryūhei, although indeed homonyms in Japanese, are in fact *all* pronounced differently in Korean as: *jang-gwan, chang-gan, song-hwan, chong-gam,* and *sang-gwan*. It is perhaps difficult to say whether the author is oblivious to this, or could not find words that are homonyms in both Japanese and Korean. Whatever the case may be, a translator of such a situation with knowledge of both Japanese and Korean must make a decision as to whether or not point out such details. In other words, the translator must prioritise based on careful consideration of relevance and project purpose. In case of this particular project, instead of separate translations for each of the five homonyms, the following single translator's note is provided:

TN: All five of the Sino-Japanese compounds listed are homonyms in Japanese pronounced '*sōkan*'. In English, this would be equivalent to something like 'air', 'heir', 'e'er', 'ere', and 'err'.

Source: example of translator's note via GMAO

As the five compounds are presumably simply listed as an example, the actual meanings of the words in Japanese are not important. The fact that the compounds are homonyms in Japanese is stated in the translator's note without putting forward an argument that would challenge the author's opinions. Finally, a similar English example of homonym is given for increased conceptual understanding.

Chapter 8: Reality of the Japan–Korea Annexation

Chapter 7, which discusses foreigner political rights in Japan, is not discussed in this chapter as the contents are of a general nature linguistically speaking. The chapter does feature some important terms, but these have already been discussed in previous sections, thus not requiring repetition. Chapter 8, the penultimate chapter (excluding epilogue and special chapter) in the publication contains a high concentration of important political and historical terms requiring discussion. The chapter is a discussion about the Japan-Korea annexation of 1910, a highly politicised historical event that is very prominent in the media and academic circles of Japan and Korea. Apart from some terms already discussed in other chapters (such as *hansei*), there are a number of historical terms in Chapter 8 that pose a challenge during translation. A few good examples are *nikkan-heigō* (Jp. 日韓併合), *ka'i-chitsujo* (Jp. 華夷秩序), *sankikyūkōtō* (Jp. 三跪九叩頭), and *gishi* (Jp. 義士).

The first term to consider is *nikkan-heigō* (Jp. 日韓併合), meaning *Japan-Korea annexation* or, more literally, *Japan-Korea amalgamation*. Use of this term has been criticised by some scholars as being deceiving and as suggesting that the events of 1910 were done by force as opposed to a "peaceful annexation/amalgamation" of two states. Nevertheless, the term most commonly used in the Korean language to refer to the event is *Hanil habbyeong* (Kr. 한일합병, 韓日合倂), the order of Japan-Korea reversed to Korea-Japan, and the characters for annexation/amalgamation are also reversed (this word, however, still carries the same meaning). The most commonly used Japanese and Korean terms are, thus, essentially the same, the only difference being the order of countries listed. This reversal (i.e., *Japan-Korea* to *Korea-Japan*) is, however, a very common phenomenon, governments generally choosing to list their own countries first (a further example would be the *Japan-South Korea World Cup*, which is known as the *South Korea-Japan World Cup* in South Korea). In the translation at hand, care was taken to retain ST word-usage wherever possible and/or appropriate, thus, naturally, the *Japan-Korea* order was used (the same choice would have been made had this been a Japanese – Korean translation, as although it is normal to reverse the order in Korean, the purpose of the translation is to maintain ST form as opposed to domesticating the text). *Nikkan-heigō* was thus translated simply as *Japan-Korea Annexation*, with no translator's notes as the event is described in good detail in the ST (and, thus, also TT). *Japan-Korea Annexation* is the most commonly used, 'neutral' option in English, less charged than, for example, *Japanese annexation of Korea* or, as it is sometimes rendered, *Japanese invasion of Korea*.

Another term requiring mention is *ka'i-chitsujo* (Jp. 華夷秩序). The first part of the compound, *ka'i* (Jp. 華夷) is a term that was used during the Ming and Qing dynasties to refer to China and foreign states (from the perspective of China), the character *ka* meaning used to represent China, whilst also meaning *flower* and *beauty/refinement*. The character *i* (used to refer to foreign states) literally means *barbarian*. The 'dichotomy' is part of an old Confucian concept whereby states that showed allegiance to the Ming and Qing Empires were seen as more advanced (Jp. *ka*, 華) than states that were not, thus, by default, becoming labelled *barbaric* (Jp. *i*, 夷). *Chitsujo*, a standard term, can mean both *order* (as in *public order*) and *system*, implying both that there was *order* based on the aforementioned idea of Chinese superiority, as well as the need for vassal states to conform to this hierarchy. Show of allegiance (and suzerainty) was achieved through regular official visits to pay tribute to the Ming/Qing emperor (discussed in more detail in the following paragraphs in relation to a further term).

The term *ka'i-chitsujo* (or *ka'i*, for that matter) is not readily found in English translation. The *Wikipedia English-Japanese Kyoto Related Comparative Translation Corpus* (2017) defines *ka'i* as "China and foreign countries (from the perspective of China); civilized and uncivilized land". Examples of *ka'i-chitsujo* in translation interestingly involve Korea: "These acts will disturb the Chinese Suzerainty over Korea" (Jp. *sonoyōna kōi ha ka'i-chitsujo wo midasu kōi dearu*, そのような行為は華夷秩序を乱す行為である). The interesting detail to note here is that the example sentence (ST) does not actually explicitly list Joseon (or Korea) in any form, suggesting that the corpus example originates from a document mentioning Korea. A more literal translation of the above ST would be: "Such acts would disturb the China-Foreign state order". It may be assumed that the ST mentions Korea contextually, in previous sentences. The previously listed translation is a good example of a domesticating approach in that it seeks an eloquent end-result in the form of a sophisticated sounding TT. The translation, however, is less useful when trying to analysis the ST or utilise it as a primary source, as is the case with the translation project at hand.

A more literal approach would be to translate *ka'i-chitsujo* as *China-Foreign state order*, however the stark contrast of the characters *ka* and *i* discussed earlier ("advanced" vs "barbaric"), which is very clear in the ST, would be lost. Ultimately, a decision was made to translate the term as the *China-Barbarian Order* with the following translator's note:

TN: 'China-Barbarian Order' (Jp. *ka'i-chitsujo*, 華夷秩序) refers to an old Confucian ideology whereby China and foreign states were deemed as part of a spectrum with China (then Ming and later Qing Empires) seen as the most culturally advanced and states that did not show allegiance through respect in the form of regular official visits, as 'barbarian'. The character used to refer to China ('*ka*') also means 'refined/beautiful' whilst the second character used to refer to foreign, non-aligned states ('*i*') means 'barbarian'.

Source: example of translator's note via GMAO

The previous translator's note helps TT readers understand the concept, as well as introducing the ST term for reference purposes. Doing so achieves both TT readability and retention of important ST information (formal historical terms).

A term that is used in the same context as *ka'i-chitsujo* is *sanki-kyūkōtō* (Jp. 三跪九叩頭). The term is used to refer to a custom from the Qing Dynasty whereby allegiance was shown to the Qing Emperor by representatives from suzerain states through a formal bow involving kneeling and then bowing three times until the head touched the ground and then repeating the process three times to a total of nine (the English expression "to kowtow" shares the same etymology). As opposed to *ka'i-chitsujo*, however, the term *sanki-kyūkōtō* is accompanied by a note from the author of the ST defining the term:

ST: ＊三跪九叩頭（さんききゅうこうとう）．．．．．．中国皇帝に対する礼儀作法の一つ。ひざまずいて、地に着くまで三回頭を下げて忠誠を誓う。これを三回くり返す。

TT: ＊'Three kneelings and nine bows': *sanki-kyūkōtō* (Jp. 三跪九叩頭)．．．．．．A rule of etiquette for use towards the emperor of China. It involves swearing allegiance by kneeling and bowing until the head touches the ground three times. This is repeated three times.

Source: (Japanese ST) *Manga Kenkanryū*, (English TT) *HH: The Comic*, p. 209

The previous explanation from the ST author is detailed enough to allow for the omitting of a translator's note. Although the note from the author does not mention that the *sanki-kyūkōtō* was exclusive to the Qing Dynasty (1636–1912), the information is given in the speech bubble first introducing the term:

ST: 当時の朝鮮は清に＊三跪九叩頭する属国に過ぎず

TT: At the time, Joseon was no more than a suzerain state of Qing which offered three kneelings and nine bows*.

Source: (Japanese ST) *Manga Kenkanryū*, (English TT) *HH: The Comic*, p. 209

The previous sentence simply lists *sanki-kyūkōtō* in Chinese characters with an asterisk linking to the author's explanation of the term (accompanied by Japanese reading in brackets). During translation, the choice was used to employ a calqued-translation in the main body of the text ('three kneelings and nine bows') with special care so as not to refer to *kōtō* as *kowtow*, as these are false-friends, the main usage of *kowtow* in English of course being "to act in an excessively subservient manner" (*Oxford*, 2005). In the author's explanatory note, the term is then defined together with the ST form (Chinese characters) and Japanese reading. Doing so achieves contextual coherence as well as the maintenance of the general form found within the ST.

The final term requiring close analysis in Chapter 8 is *gishi* (Jp. 義士), which some Japanese-English dictionaries list as: "a loyal (devoted) retainer; an upright person; a person of principles; a righteous warrior; a samurai" (*Kenkyūsha*, 2008). In the ST, the term is used by the protagonist's 'friend/rival(?)' Matsumoto Kōichi (a '*zainichi* Korean') in reference to An Jung-Geun, a Korean who assassinated the then (1909) Prime Minister of Japan, Itō Hirobumi:

ST: その頃は、安重根義士のような日帝の支配に抵抗した英雄もいるんだ！！

TT: During that time, there was even a hero like the righteous warrior An Jung-Geun who opposed the Japanese Empire's rule!!

Source: (Japanese ST) *Manga Kenkanryū*, (English TT – Draft) *HH: The Comic*, p. 211

The previous translation, utilising *righteous warrior*, although not problematic at first glance, does not capture the contextual, linguistic 'quirk' of Kōichi's statement. The term *gishi* is seldom used in Japanese, particularly when compared to the Korean language. Korean utilises the same Chinese compound (Kr. *wisa*, 의사) as Japanese, the term often used as an honorary title for Korean independence fighters who fought against the Japanese Empire.

The meaning, however, is more complex than simply *righteous warrior*, as it is semantically equal to *martyr*. This equivalence may be confirmed with the help of a Korean-English dictionary: 'a righteous person; a martyr' (*Dong-A*, 2005). *Martyr* does appear as a translation for *gishi* in Japanese, however only through a back-translation from the English (and only in some dictionaries) and even then only as part of an example sentence: "a martyr to a cause; a martyr to science; He became the martyr of liberty" (*Kenkyūsha*, 2008). The more commonly available (i.e., readily accessible) term in Japanese is *junkyōsha* (Jp. 殉教者), however this is only used in contexts where there are religious grounds for martyrdom (as opposed to non-religious ideology or ideals as well as metaphorical usage, as is the case in the ST). The choice was thus made to translate the sentence with *gishi* as:

ST: その頃は、安重根義士のような日帝の支配に抵抗した英雄もいるんだ！！

TT: During that time, there was even a hero like martyr An Jung-Geun who opposed the Japanese Empire's rule!!

Source: (Japanese ST) *Manga Kenkanryū*, (English TT – Final) *HH: The Comic*, p. 211

It should be noted that the translation of *gishi* in this context as *martyr* is particularly important as, as mentioned earlier, Kōichi's usage of the term is non-standard in Japanese (and certainly not the 'go-to' term available when translating from Japanese to English) and a defining feature in his character building as a '*zainichi* Korean', as the term is commonly used by Korean speakers with reference to An Jung-Geun.

Chapter 9: Invasion of Japanese Territory – The Takeshima Problem + Epilogue & Special

The final, official chapter of *Manga Kenkanryū*, Chapter 9, discusses the heated territorial dispute surrounding Liancourt Rocks (known as

Takeshima in Japanese and Dokdo in Korean). The publication is then concluded with an 'epilogue' about what needs to happen for 'Japan-South Korea friendship' to be achieved, and a 'special' about the then (2005) boom surrounding the South Korean soap opera, *Winter Sonata* (Kr. *Gyeoul Yeonga*, 겨울연가; Jp. *Fuyu no Sonata*, 冬のソナタ). Although neither the chapter nor the additional contents are particularly complex, there are two issues that required some consideration during translation. Namely, *Liancourt Rocks* and terms from the Korean language such as the verb ending *nida*.

As mentioned throughout this work, in a translation project which is meant to create a source for further research and inquiry, it is important to consider all implications of word choice and layout for the sake of maintaining (or trying to maintain) neutrality. When translating content relating to disputed issues such as the Liancourt Rocks problem, this can lead to some difficult choices. Seemingly benign choices, such as listing 'Takeshima (Islands)' before 'Dokdo (Islands)' or 'Korea' before 'Japan' when defining a dispute or issue in an English translator's note may, potentially, lead to criticism (i.e., favouritism on part of the translator) from either side of the spectrum. Dealing with such (dis)orderly issue is particularly difficult in the case of the Liancourt Rocks dispute, as the body of land happens to be located in a body of water between the two aforementioned nations, the name of which is also currently disputed as either the *Sea of Japan* or the *East Sea* (once again, such listing becomes unavoidable).

In this project, the choice has been made to list such proper nouns in whichever order they were listed in the ST. This, of course, only solves half of the problem, as translator's notes come from the translator and not the ST author. In a project where 'neutrality' is tentatively mentioned, the impossibility of the task becomes all the more apparent.

The issue directly relates to the 'impossibility' of translation and ideas discussed in relation to Deconstruction in Chapter 4 and a never-ending chain of signified-signifier that is seemingly impossible to decode – or as Mona Baker (2006) may say – a 'narrative' that cannot be escaped. The aim of this project, however, is to side-step the 'impossible'. The use of GMAO allows for side-by-side existence of the ST and TT pair, as well as additional content from the translator in the form of translator's notes. The multiplicity of the act of translation is, therefore, in full view – including all of the translator's imperfections and reasoning behind translation choices. The aim of the project is empirical – so as to further discussion and debate. This may be made possible through action (as discussed in previous chapters, *not* translating is not an option that should be taken).

This leads to the need for choice. It is not always possible to avoid listing in, for example, translator's notes. A viable option is to notify readers of one's intentions – this may be achieved through a foreword, such as is the case in the current project:

Disclaimer from the Translator

I created the following translation of Manga Kenkanryū (authored by Sharin Yamano) for the purpose of utilisation as a primary source for research and inquiry. I have translated the publication to the best of my ability as someone from an Asian Studies and Translation Studies background with fluency in the Japanese and Korean languages. The translation is also an example of a new approach utilising Great Manga Application Onidzuka (GMAO). Whilst the application is an excellent tool when dealing with the translation of visual material, it may also be used in the translation of various other types of publications, perhaps particularly those relating to controversial issues in fields such as history and politics.

It should be noted that maintaining 'absolute neutrality' in translation is ultimately impossible, as reader reception is something that cannot be controlled by writers. In the translation of debated terms, I have strived to use neutral terms and/or most widely available translations. It should be noted that terms dominant in the source text have been as per the source text (for example, 'Japan and Korea' as opposed to 'Korea and Japan', even if the latter is the norm in English). This choice (for example, listing Japan first) is not meant to reflect on my own personal beliefs in relation to issues in East Asia. I am a strong supporter of dialogue and discussion, something which I believe can only be achieved when more than one party are present. Making a range of sources from languages other than English available is one of the first steps.

Source: translator's disclaimer from *Hate Hallyu: The Comic*

The previous translator's disclaimer, which would appear as the initial screen when opening GMAO, provides readers with a very explicit message listing the translation/project purpose, as well as the translator's intended separation from the ST discourse itself. Using a translator's note, the listing of proper nouns such as the names of countries is given as an example of an inevitable choice that has to be made for the sake of form as well as the very 'existence' of the translator. Ironically, such an action is something that can also lead to the translator's 'demise', but it is part of an empirical choice and (pro)activism.

The final issue discussed in this chapter is satirical addition of the Korean verb ending *nida* and use of other Korean language phrases as in the following examples:

ST: 竹島？知らないニダ (p. 248)
 Romanisation: Takeshima? Shiranai'nida
 ST: ウリの優秀な文化にひれふすニダ (p. 278)
 Romanisation: Uri no yūshūna bunka ni hirefusu'nida
 ST: ケンチャナヨ〜 (p. 285)
 Romanisation: *Kenchanayo~*

Source: examples of Korean from *Manga Kenkanryū*, pp. 248, 278, 285

In the first two examples, sentences in Japanese are concluded with the polite Korean verb ending *nida* (Kr. 니다) transcribed in *katakana*. As discussed earlier in the chapter, *katakana* script is used for loan words as well as emphasis. In this case, it is most likely a case of both (the characters using the expression are portrayed as Korean, something that is made evident with context and drawing style. The second example also includes the Korean word *uri* meaning *our* (which also features in "Far East Asia Investigation Committee Report: File 03 – The realities of South Korean fabrication/copying"), also in *katakana*. The third example *kenchanayo* is a Japanese transcription of the Korean phrase *gwaen'chanayo* (Kr. 괜찮아요) meaning *it's ok* or *all right/no problem*.

In case of the *nida*, *uri*, and *kenchanayo* differences in Japanese/Korean and English grammar make for unnatural direct transfer (i.e., attaching *nida* to the end of an English sentence as in '*I don't know-nida*' for '*shiranai-nida*'). What is more, as Japanese readers tend to be more exposed to the Korean language when compared to English background speakers, the impact is different (most Japanese readers will know the meaning of *nida* and *kenchanayo*). Achieving the exact same impact, however, is not the purpose of the translation. In theory, a similar impact may be achieved by conjuring a sentence using what is perceived as awkward sounding English based on certain stereotypes. Although such an approach may be acceptable in a translation aimed for, say, popular consumption (where similar comic effect, for example, carries greater importance), the project aim here is to adhere closely to the ST with restricted manipulation of ST form and message.

Translating *nida* using a domesticating approach using stereotypes from the English-speaking world would, thus, go against the project purpose and, in addition, place the translator in danger of being perceived as racist do to undue creativity from the view of TT readers and, potentially, the ST author who may later argue that the use of *nida* is simply there for the emphasis of the 'Korean'ness' of the characters. Indeed, what is socially acceptable varies greatly from culture to culture – most readers of Japanese would not perceive the use of *nida*, *uri*, or *kenchanayo* as racist, whereas the same would not be the case with stereotypical speech in an English text. Conveying culture-bound social norms is a difficult matter that would in most cases involve the translator superimposing their own values, which, although bound to happen to some extent anyway, can be controlled to a certain point.

In light of this, the most appropriate method of translating Korean words was deemed to be leaving the term as is (in the case of *nida*, at the end of an English translation of the Japanese sentence) with a brief translator's note informing readers of the origins of the terms as follows:

TN: '*nida*' (Jp. ニダ) is a polite Korean verb ending (Kr. *nida*, 니다) equivalent to '*masu*' (Jp. ます) in Japanese.

TN: '*Uri*' (Jp. ウリ) is a Korean word (Kr. 우리) meaning 'our', equivalent to the Japanese '*uchi*' (Jp. うち) or '*waga*' (Jp. 我が).

TN: '*Kenchanayo*' is a Korean phrase (Kr. 괜찮아요) meaning 'it's ok' or 'all right/no problem' equivalent to the Japanese '*daijōbu*' (Jp. 大丈夫).

Source: example of translator's notes via GMAO

Notes

1 Although an 'honorific' suffix, *san* may also be used with plain (*futsūtai*) and even informal (*tameguchi*) language, as usage is more to do with sociolinguistics and hierarchy than actual 'respect'.
2 Chinese and other languages that use Chinese background vocabulary, such as Vietnamese, utilise the same or similar word choice as Japanese, with their own native pronunciation (e.g., the Korean Peninsula in Mandarin Chinese is *Cháoxiǎn Bàndǎo* (Ch. 朝鮮半島) and *Bán đảo Triều Tiên* (半島朝鮮) in Vietnamese.

3 *Minkoku/Minguk* (Jp. 民国, Kr. 民國) itself is a South Korean variant of the word *republic* (normally referred to in Japanese and Korean as 共和国/共和 國, Jp. *Kyōwakoku*, Kr. *Gonghwaguk*, respectively), first proposed as a suffix to *Daikan/Daehan* during the Korean independence movement of 1919 (Song, 2013).

4 For additional mention about the Korean publications, see *Ken-Honyaku-Ryū: Issues in the Translation of Controversial Texts Focusing on the Manga Comics Hate Hallyu: The Comic and Hate Japanese Wave* (Zulawnik, 2016).

5 The faction identified with may be pre-colonial period *unified Joseon, South/North Korea* or simply *Korea*. Third generation Korean background Japanese poet/ writer-translator Zhong Zhang, for example, prefers to refer to himself as '*saramu*' (Jp. サラム Kr. 사람, *saram*), simply meaning *person* or *human* (Zhong, 2009).

7   Conclusion

The outcomes of the project described in this book may be divided in to two main categories: a broad theoretical and methodological framework proposing technologically assisted multi-modal translation in an augmented environment and the exemplification of this process through the translation of the graphic novel *Hate Hallyu: The Comic*. These two primary outcomes may be then expanded further across a number of applicable disciplines.

The project framework and methodology, exemplified through the translation of *Manga Kenkanryū*, offers an opportunity for the development of a program based on GMAO that may be hosted on an augmented online translation space. Such a translation space – or hub – may be used to translate and research multi-modal texts such as graphic novels, advertising, and image. At the same time, the program and space hosting it may act as a pedagogical and training tool within translation, applicable both in academic and professional settings. Specifically, the program may be developed so as to provide additional resources to users, translators, academics, and students alike. Potential improvements may include categorised annotations, hyperlinks to external resources including dictionaries and corpora, and compatibility with existing CAT tools such as TRADOS.

The benefits of such an expanded, multi-modal approach are numerous. In an academic setting, increased visibility of the translator allows for critical analysis and discussion relating to translation choices and translator reasoning and decision making. The benefits to readers come in the form of increased appreciation of the translated discourse in respect of the source and target text pair and the subtleties and complexity of the translation task itself. In a more general setting, a developed translation space and reader/consumer-oriented interface for access to multi-modal translations of such media as graphic novels (and many others, such as advertising and visual encyclopaedias) would increase interest in the medium as well as source cultures and the difficult task that is translation. In other words, there is outlook for academic and popular applications, both of which have the

DOI: 10.4324/9781003167792-7

potential for raising awareness not only about the issues discussed in the source texts and source text cultures but also the importance of the translator and translation process.

In terms of discipline specific outcomes, the resulting scholarly English translation of *Manga Kenkanryū* (Yamano, 2005) may offer insights into discourse pertaining to animosity within Japan-South Korea relations as seen in the popular medium that is the graphic novel. Yamano's (2005) publication is a seminal work when considering Japanese anti-Korean sentiments stemming from the appearance and apparent rise in domestic popularity of South Korean popular culture (*Hallyu* aka the Korean Wave) since around the turn of the 21st century. Analysis of such texts may lead to deeper, better-informed discussion and mediation based on increased research on relevant discourse. As mentioned earlier, there is potential for expansion of annotations to include hyperlinks to further external sources such as word-databases, dictionaries, encyclopaedias, academic articles, encryption of sound files so as to help in the understanding of onomatopoeia, and any other additional information the translator may see as relevant to meeting their specific project purpose.

The translation microanalytically addresses text-specific linguistic issues such as the translation of controversial political and historical discourse, providing insight into the difficulty surrounding such translation tasks. Considering the controversial nature of the source text, the project methodology and resulting text are also an example of certain proposed risk mitigation elements including vastly increased translator/translation visibility and responsibility. Thus, both the translated text and the translator may be a source of research beneficial to fields such as translation studies, history, Japanese/Korean studies, and politics. Although the task of translating heated discourse 'risk-free' is difficult, the method proposed as part of my work is a real way of making the translator visible, and it may have any number of benefits such as reducing risk, pedagogical application, linguistic interest, cultural studies, and awareness and appreciation of translation and the translator.

There is great potential for further research, particularly in regard to the development of a program modelled around GMAO – the creation of an augmented translation space. The next step in such research should be the development of a new program with increased capabilities and function, both in respect of the translator and readership. There is real potential for the development of both academic/professional and general use applications: an extended academic/professional program which may be part of an online learning network for the translation and evaluation of multi-modal texts and translator education, and a separate public application divided into a translation program and a viewing platform for accessing expanded multi-modal translations. I sincerely hope that my work will spark greater interest in the analysis of 'controversial' materials and 'contraverse', as I term it, in general, as I believe that it may be the key to greater contextual understanding and, as a result, peace without the need to wrap oneself in white bed linen.

Bibliography

Akbari, M. (2009). Risk management in translation. In H. Che Omar, H. Haroon, & A. Abd Ghani (Eds.), *The sustainability of the translation field. The 12th international conference of translation* (pp. 209–218). Kuala Kumpur: Malaysian Translators Association.

Àlvarez, M., & Vidal, C. A. (Eds.). (1996). *Translation, power, subversion. Translating: A political act* (pp. 1–9). Clevedon; Philadelphia; Adelaide: Multilingual Matters.

Apter, E. (2006). *The translation zone: A new comparative literature*. Princeton, NJ and Oxford: Princeton University Press.

Baker, M. (2006). *Translation and conflict*. London: Taylor & Francis Publishing.

Baker, M. (2010). Reframing conflict in translation. In M. Baker (Ed.), *Critical readings in translation studies*. London and New York, NY: Routledge.

Bassnett, S. (1996). The meek or the mighty: Reappraising the role of the translator. In M. Àlvarez & C. A. Vidal (Eds.), *Translation, power, subversion* (pp. 10–24). Clevedon; Philadelphia; Adelaide: Multilingual Matters.

Bassnett, S., & Lefevere, A. (Eds.). (1990). *Translation, history, and culture*. London and New York, NY: Routledge.

Baudinette, T. (2016). An evaluation of physicality in the bara manga of Bádi magazine. In S. Pasfield-Neofitou & C. Sell (Eds.), *Manga vision* (pp. 107–124). Melbourne: Monash University Press.

Beckett, S. (1953). *L'Innommable (The Unnamable)*. Paris: Les Éditions de Minuit.

Beckett, S. (2006). The lost ones. In *The Grove centenary edition of the complete works of Samuel Beckett* (Vol. 3, pp. 381–399). New York, NY: Grove Press.

Bell, C. (2016). From victim to kira: Death Note and the misplaced agencies of cosmic justice. In S. Pasfield-Neofitou & C. Sell (Eds.), *Manga vision* (pp. 70–86). Melbourne: Monash University Press.

Bellos, D. (2012). *Is that a fish in your ear?: The amazing adventure of translation*. New York, NY: Penguin Books.

British Broadcasting Corporation (BBC) (2013). *Bavaria Abandons plans for new edition of Mein Kampf*. Retrieved January 26, 2021, from www.bbc.com/news/world-europe-25346140

British Broadcasting Corporation (BBC) (2016a). *Copyright of Hitler's Mein Kampf expires*. Retrieved January 26, 2021, from www.bbc.com/news/world-europe-35209185

British Broadcasting Corporation (BBC) (2016b). *Mein Kampf hits stores in tense Germany*. Retrieved January 26, 2021, from www.bbc.com/news/world-europe-35242523

British Broadcasting Corporation (BBC) World Service. (2011). *BBC World Service Poll, EMBARGO 00:01 GMT 07 March 2011*. Retrieved August 5, 2021, from http://news.bbc.co.uk/2/shared/bsp/hi/pdfs/05_03_11_bbcws_country_poll.pdf

British Broadcasting Corporation (BBC) World Service. (2012). *BBC Word Service Poll, EMBARGO 23:01 GMT 10 May 2012*. Retrieved August 5, 2021, from www.worldpublicopinion.org/pipa/pdf/may12/BBCEvals_May12_rpt.pdf

British Broadcasting Corporation (BBC) World Service. (2013). *BBC Word Service Poll, EMBARGO 23:01 GMT 22 May 2013*. Retrieved August 5, 2021, from www.worldpublicopinion.org/pipa/2013%20Country%20Rating%20Poll.pdf

Buden, B. (2006). *Translation is impossible! Let's do it!* European Institute for Progressive Cultural Policies. Retrieved March 31, 2017 from http://eipcp.net/transversal/1206/buden/en

Cheetham, D. (2010). Translating direction: Illustrations in native and translated Japanese children's literature. In *International research in children's literature* (Vol. 3, pp. 44–60). Edinburgh: Edinburgh University Press.

Cheong, S. (1991). *The politics of anti-Japanese sentiment in Korea: Japanese-South Korean relations under American occupation, 1945–1952*. Santa Barbara, CT: Greenwood Press.

Chesterman, A., & Wagner, E. (2002). *Can theory help translators? A dialogue between the ivory tower and the wordface*. Manchester: St. Jerome Publishing.

Choe, G. S. (2003). 일본과 임진왜란 [*Japan and the imjin war*]. Seoul: Korea University Press.

Choe, G. S. (2014). 韓国の米軍慰安婦はなぜ生まれたのか [*What created the American Army's South Korean comfort women?*]. Tokyo: Heart Publishing.

Choe, N. S. (1997). 조선 상식 문답 [朝鮮常識問答] [*Common knowledge about Joseon*]. Seoul: Minsokwon. (Original work published 1946)

Choi, S. (2010). 김치애국주의 [*Kimchi patriotism*]. Seoul: Inmulgwasasangsa.

Chomsky, N. (2015). *Because we say so*. London: Penguin Books.

Chosun Ilbo. (2011, August 22). *Japanese March against Korean soap operas*. Retrieved August 5, 2021, from http://english.chosun.com/site/data/html_dir/2011/08/22/2011082200679.html

Cintas, D. (2012). The manipulation of audiovisual translation. *Meta, 57*.

Davis, K. (2001). *Deconstruction and translation* (pp. 28–29, 49–66). Manchester: St. Jerome Publishing.

Delisle, J., Lee-Jahnke, H., & Cormier, M. C. (1999). *Translation terminology* (p. 179). Amsterdam: John Benjamins Publishing Company.

Derrida, J. (2001). What is a 'Relevant' Translation? (L. Venuti Trans.). In *Critical Enquiry* (Vol. 27, pp. 174–200). Chicago, IL: The University of Chicago Press.

DigitalDaijisen(ディジタル大辞泉)(2022).*Keyword:「韓流」(kanryū)*.Retrieved January 18, 2018, from http://dic.yahoo.co.jp/dsearch?enc=UTF-8&p=%E9%9F%93%E6%B5%81&dtype=0&dname=0na&stype=0&pagenum=1&index=21307900

Ducke, I. (2002). *Status power: Japan's foreign policy towards South Korea*. New York, NY: Routledge.

Duus, P. (1998). *The abacus and the sword: The Japanese penetration of Korea, 1895–1910.* Berkeley, CA: California University Press.

East Asia Institute. (2013). *Japan-South Korea joint public opinion poll.* Retrieved August 5, 2021, from www.genron-npo.net/en/opinion_polls/archives/5263.html

East Asia Institute. (2014). *Japan-South Korea joint public opinion poll.* Retrieved August 5, 2021, from www.genron-npo.net/en/pp/archives/5142.html

East Asia Institute. (2015). *Japan-South Korea joint public opinion poll.* Retrieved August 5, 2021, from www.genron-npo.net/en/pp/archives/5183.html

East Asia Institute. (2016). *Japan-South Korea joint public opinion poll.* Retrieved August 5, 2021, from www.genron-npo.net/en/opinion_polls/archives/5305.html

East Asia Institute. (2017). *Japan-South Korea joint public opinion poll.* Retrieved August 5, 2021, from www.genron-npo.net/en/opinion_polls/archives/5365.html

El Shiekh, A. A. A. (2012). Translation: Bridging the gap, or creating a gap to bridge? Reflections on the role of translation in bridging and/or widening the gap between different cultures with particular reference to religion and politics. *International Journal of English Linguistics, 2*(1), 28–33.

European Union. (2018). *Translation and multilingualism.* Retrieved July 20, 2018 from https://publications.europa.eu/en/publication-detail/-/publication/e0770e72-afa1-4971-8824-6190512537dc/language-en

Fazzo, D. L. (1991, July 4). Tradusse 'Versetti ōanici' Un Iraniano Lo Accoltella. *Cronaca.* Retrieved October 8, 2021, from http://ricerca.repubblica.it/repubblica/archivio/repubblica/1991/07/04/tradusse-versetti-satanici-un-iraniano-lo-accoltella.html

Fukuda, H. (1993). *Flip, slither & Bang-Japanese sound and action words.* Tokyo: Kodansha International.

Genette, G. (1997). *Paratexts: Thresholds of interpretation* (J. E. Lewin, Trans., Foreword by R. Macksey). Cambridge: Cambridge University Press.

Gentzler, E., & Tymoczko, M. (Eds.). (2002). *Translation and power.* Amherst: University of Massachusetts Press.

Hart-Landsberg, M. (1998). *Korea: Division, reunification, and U.S. foreign policy.* Washington, DC: Monthly Review Press.

Hatim, B. (Ed.). (2001). *Teaching and researching translation* (pp. 73–80). Manchester: Pearson Education Limited.

Hatim, B. (2009). Translating text in context. In J. Munday (Ed.), *The Routledge companion to translation studies* (1st ed., pp. 36–53). London: Routledge.

Hermans, T. (1999). *Translation in systems: Descriptive and system-oriented approaches explained.* Manchester: St. Jerome.

Hermans, T. (2009). Translation, ethics, politics. In J. Munday (Ed.), *The Routledge companion to translation studies* (1st ed., pp. 93–105). London: Routledge.

Hiraga, M. K. (2006). Kanji: The visual metaphor. *Style, 40*(1–2).

Hitler, A. (1925). *Mein Kampf [My struggle].* Munich: Eher-Verlag.

Holton, B. (2014). Dubbing Du Fu: Paratext and hypertext. In V. Pellatt (Ed.), *Text, extratext, metatext and paratext in translation* (pp. 121–126). Newcastle upon Tyne: Cambridge Scholars Publishing.

Holz-Mänttäri, J. (1986). *Translatorisches Handeln: Theorie und Methode.* Helsinki: Suomalainen Tiedeakademia. (Original work published 1984)

Hou, P. (2014). Paratexts in the translation of the selected works of Mao Tse-tung. In V. Pellatt (Ed.), *Text, extratext, metatext and paratext in translation* (pp. 33–48). Newcastle upon Tyne: Cambridge Scholars Publishing.

House, J. (1977). *A model for translation quality assessment: A model revisited.* Tübingen: Guunter Narr.

Hulbert, H. (1905). *The history of Korea* (Vol. 1 and 2). Seoul: The Methodist Publishing House.

Hwang, M., & Shin, D. (1993). 醜い韓国人を書いた醜い日本人 [*The Ugly Japanese who wrote 'Ugly South Koreans'*]. Tokyo: Takarajima.

Inose, H. (2008). Translating Japanese onomatopoeia and mimetic words. In A. Pym & A. Perekrestenko (Eds.), *Intercultural studies group, Universitat Rovira i Virgili Translation research projects 1* (pp. 97–116). Retrieved October 15, 2021, from http://isg.urv.es/library/papers/InoseOnomatopoeia.pdf

Itagaki, R. (2007a). マンガ嫌韓流と人種主義―国民主義の構造 [Manga Kenkanryū and ethnocentrism – The structure of nationalism]. *Zenya, 11*(1), 20–34.

Itagaki, R. (2007b). 嫌韓流の何が問題か―歴史教育・メディア・消費文化・戦争とレイシズム[What is the problem with Kenkanryū? Historical education, media, consumerist culture, war and racism]. *Zenya, 11*(1), 35–45.

Japan Times. (2016). Record 2.38 million foreign residents living in Japan in 2016. Retrieved February 4, 2018, from www.japantimes.co.jp/news/2017/03/17/national/record-2-38-million-foreign-residents-living-japan-2016/#.WnaJokxuLIV

Jeong, Y. T. (2005, July 18). 일 인터넷서점서 한국 혐오 만화 예매 1위 [Korea-hating *manga* #1 order in Japanese internet book shop]. *SBS*. Retrieved August 21, 2017, from http://news.naver.com/main/read.nhn?mode=LSD&mid=sec&sid1=103&oid=096&aid=0000021333

Jüngst, H. (2008a). Translating Manga. In F. Zanettin (Ed.), *Comics in translation* (pp. 50–78). Manchester and New York, NY: St. Jerome Publishing.

Jüngst, H. (2008b). Translating educational comics. In F. Zanettin (Ed.), *Comics in translation* (pp. 172–199). Manchester and New York, NY: St. Jerome Publishing.

Kaindl, K. (1999). Thump, whizz, boom: A framework for the study of comics under translation. *Target, 11*(2), 263–288.

Kamigaito, K. (2004). 文禄・慶長の役 [*The first and second Japanese invasions of Joseon*]. Tokyo: Kodansha. (Original work published 2002)

Katan, D. (2018). 'Free, free, set them free. . .': What deconstraining subtitles can do for AVT. In I. Ranzato & S. Zanotti (Eds.), *Linguistic and cultural representation in audiovisual translation*. London and New York, NY: Routledge.

Kess, J. F., & Miyamoto, T. (1999). *The Japanese mental lexicon*. Philadelphia, PA: John Benjamins.

Kim, M. G., et al. (2000). 우리 민족해방운동사 [*The history of our race's independence movement*]. Seoul: Yeoksabipyeongsa.

Kim, G. D. (2000). 한반도의 분단과 전쟁 [*Division and war on the Korean Peninsula*]. Seoul: Seoul University Press.

Kim, G. H. (2010). 망국의 역사 조선을 읽다 [*The history of a destroyed nation – Reading Joseon*]. Seoul: Dolbegae.

Kim, J. H. (1999). 한일관계의 구조와 특성 [The structure and characteristics of South Korea-Japan relations]. In D. J. Kim et al. (Eds.), 한국의 외교정책 [*South Korea's foreign policy*] (pp. 401–415). Seoul: Oreum.

Kim, S. H. (2011, January 13). 혐한류 왜 나오나? [What is the reason behind Hate Korean Wave?]. *Hankook Ilbo*. Retrieved March 1, 2017, from http://news.hankooki.com/ArticleView/ArticleViewSH.php?url=music/201101/sp2011011317544595510.htm&cd=2203&ver=v002

Kim, Y. S. (2013). 임진왜란 비겁한 승리 [*The imjin war – A cowardly victory*]. Seoul: Aelpi.

Kim, Y. U. (1989). 한-일 민족의 원형: 같은 씨에서 다른꽃이 핀다 [*Original form of the Korean/Japanese peoples – A different flower blooms from the same seed*]. Seoul: Pyeongminsa.

Kitajima, M. (2012). 秀吉の朝鮮侵略と民衆 [*The masses and Hideyoshi's invasion of Joseon*]. Tokyo: Iwanami Shoten.

Lakoff, G., & Johnson, M. (1980). *Metaphors we live by*. Chicago, IL: University of Chicago Press.

Larson, M. L. (1998). *Meaning-based translation – A guide to cross-language equivalence* (2nd ed., pp. 17–25). New York, NY: University Press of America.

Lee, C. (2006). *Popular culture, Korea and Japanese national identity:* Fuyu no Sonata *and* Kenkanryū (Unpublished honour's thesis). Melbourne: Asia Institute, The University of Melbourne.

Lee, C. H. (2012, August 10). 日보수매체 "한류반대 시위는 차별주의" 비판 [Conservative Japanese media criticise anti-Korean Wave protests as "racist"]. *Yonhap News*. Retrieved August 20, 2021, from http://news.naver.com/main/read.nhn?mode=LSD&mid=sec&sid1=104&oid=001&aid=0005750112

Lee, J., & Moon, C. (2002). Responding to Japan's Asia policy: The Korean calculus. In I. Takashi (Ed.), *Japan's Asian policy: Revival and response*. New York, NY: Palgrave Macmillan.

Lee, J. Y. (2011, August 10). 혐한류와 청년 백수 [Hate Korean wave and the idle youth]. *Dong-a*. Retrieved August 11, 2021, from http://news.donga.com/3/all/20110810/39426629/1

Lefevere, A. (1985). Why waste our time on rewrites?: The trouble with interpretation and the role of rewriting in an alternative paradigm. In T. Hermans (Ed.), *The manipulation of literature*. London: Routledge.

Lefevere, A. (1992). *Translation, rewriting an the manipulation of literary fame*. London and New York, NY: Routledge.

Leppihalme, R. (1994). Translating allusions: When minimum change is not enough. *Target*, *6*(2).

Lim, I., & Zulawnik, A. (2021). *Interviews with North Korean Defectors: From Kim Shin-jo to Thae Yong-ho* (1st ed.). London; New York: Routledge. https://doi.org/10.4324/9781003152941

Liscutin, N. (2009). Surfing the neo-nationalist wave: A case study of Manga Kenkanryū. In C. Berry, N. Liscutin, & J. D. Mackintosh (Eds.), *Cultural studies and cultural industries in Northeast Asia-what a difference a region makes* (pp. 171–193). Hong Kong: Hong Kong University Press.

Maier, C. (2007). The translator as an intervenient being. In J. Munday (Ed.), *Translation as intervention* (pp. 1–17). London and New York, NY: Continuum.

Massidda, S. (2015). *Audiovisual translation in the digital age: The Italian Fansubbing phenomenon*. Basingstoke: Palgrave Macmillan.

104   *Bibliography*

Mendl, W. (1995). *Japan's Asia policy: Regional security and global interests*. London and New York: Routledge.

Munday, J. (2012). *Introducing translation studies – Theories and applications* (3rd ed., pp. 119–125). Manchester: Routledge.

Nabokov, V. (2012). Problems in translation: Onegin in English. In L. Venuti (Ed.), *The translation studies reader*. London and New York, NY: Routledge. Original work published 1955

Nakano, H. (2008). 文禄・慶長の役(戦争の日本史16) [*Japan's first and second invasions of Joseon* (Japanese history of war 16)]. Tokyo: Yoshikawa Hirofumi Publishing.

Neubert, A., & Shreve, G. (1992). *Translation as text*. Kent, OH: Kent State University Press.

New York Times. (2010). *Rebuffing scholars, Germany vows to keep Hitler out of print*. Retrieved February 3, 2021, from www.nytimes.com/2010/02/05/world/europe/05germany.html

Newmark, P. (1981). *Approaches to translation*. Oxford and New York, NY: Pergamon.

Nida, E. A. (1964). *Toward a science of translating*. Leiden: Brill Academic Publishers.

Nikkan Cyzo. (2008). よしりんと戦争勃発! 佐藤優ロングインタビュー [*'Outbreak of War with Yoshirin!' A long interview with Satō Masaru*]. Retrieved August 20, 2021, from (PART A) www.cyzo.com/2008/10/post_1093.html (PART B) www.cyzo.com/2008/10/post_1094_entry.html

Nishimura, K. (2006). 反日の超克－中国、韓国、北朝鮮とどう対峙するか [*Overcoming anti-Japanese sentiment – How to confront China, South Korea, and North Korea*] (pp. 41–61). Tokyo: PHP Interface.

Nord, C. (Ed.). (2001). *Translating as a purposeful activity – Functionalist approaches explained* (2nd ed., pp. 1–38, 41–79, 109–122). Manchester: St. Jerome Publishing. (Original work published 1997)

Nord, C. (2005). *Textanalyze und Übersetzen: Theoretische Grundlagen, Methode und didaktische Anwendung einer übersetzungsrelevanten Textanalyze* [*Text analysis in translation: Theory, methodology and didactic application of a model for translation – Oriented text analysis*) (C. Nord & P. Sparrow, Trans.). Amsterdam: Rodopi (Original work published 1988).

Norris, C. (2002). *Deconstruction: Theory and practice*. New York, NY: Routledge.

Oberdorfer, D., & Carlin, R. (2013). *The two Koreas: A contemporary history*. New York, NY: Perseus.

Ogura, K. (2005). 韓流インパクト－ ルックコリアと日本の主体化 [*Korean wave impact – Look at South Korea and the subjectification of Japan*] (pp. 9–10, 52–53). Tokyo: Kodansha.

O'Hagan, M. (2006). Manga, anime and video games: Globalizing Japanese cultural production. *Perspectives*, *14*(4).

Onishi, N. (2005, November 19). Ugly images of Asian rivals become best sellers in Japan. *The New York Times*. https://www.nytimes.com/2005/11/19/world/asia/ugly-images-of-asian-rivals-become-best-sellers-in-japan.html

Park, T. H. (1993). 醜い韓国人 [*Ugly South Koreans*]. Tokyo: Kobunsha.

Park, T. H., & Kase, H. (1995). 醜い韓国人 - 歴史検証編 [*Ugly South Koreans – Historical verification edition*]. Tokyo: Kobunsha.

Park, Y. H. (2004). 반일민족주의를 넘어서 [*Getting over Anti-Japanese nationalism*]. Seoul: Sahoepyeongreon.

Park, Y. H. (2014). 제국의 위안부 [*The Comfort Women of the Empire* – 2014 refers to the Japanese edition under the same title (Jp. 帝国の慰安婦)]. Seoul: Ppuripari (Korean Ed.). Tokyo: Asahi Shimbun Publications (Japanese Ed.). (Original work published 2013)

Pasfield-Neofitou, S., & Sell, C. (Eds.). (2016). *Manga vision – Cultural and communicative perspectives*. Melbourne: Monash University Press.

Pellatt, V. (Ed.). (2014). *Text, extratext, metatext and paratext in translation* (pp. 1–8). Newcastle upon Tyne: Cambridge Scholars Publishing.

Pérez, C. (2014). *Apropos of ideology: Translation studies on ideology*. London and New York, NY: Routledge.

Petrou, M. (2010). Haunted by satanic verses. *Maclean's, 123*(23), 33.

Pym, A. (1996). Venuti's visibility (review article). *Target, 8*(1), 165–177.

Pym, A. (2010). *Text and risk in translation* (Version 2.0, pp. 1–11). Tarragona: Intercultural Studies Group, Universitat Rovira i Virgili.

Pym, A. (2012). *On translator ethics. Principles for cross-cultural communication*. Amsterdam and Philadelphia, PA: John Benjamins.

Pym, A. (2015). Translating as risk management. *Journal of Pragmatics, 85*(1), 67–80.

Pym, A. [AnthonyPym] (Host), & Even-Zohar (Discussion participant). (2012, July 16). Questions of culture: Even-Zohar, Chesterman, Pym [Video file]. Retrieved February 1, 2021, from www.youtube.com/watch?v=ktI9PVJICfk

Reiß, K. (2000). *Möglichkeiten und Grenzen der Übersetzungskritik (Translation criticism – The potentials & limitations: Categories and criteria for translation quality assessment)* (E. F. Rhodes, Trans.). Manchester: St. Jerome Publishing. (Original work published 1971)

Republic of Korea Law Portal. (2018). *Special law to redeem pro-Japanese collaborator's property*. Retrieved July 20, 2021 from http://law.go.kr/lsInfoP.do?lsiSeq=113181#0000

Robertson, W. (2016). Writing another's tongue – Orthographic representations of non-fluency in Japanese manga. In S. Pasfield-Neofitou & C. Sell (Eds.), *Manga vision* (pp. 161–177). Melbourne: Monash University Press.

Robinson, D. (1996). *Translation & taboo*. DeKalb, IL: Northern University Press.

Rota, V. (2008). Aspects of adaptation – The translation of comics formats. In F. Zanettin (Ed.), *Comics in translation* (pp. 79–98). Manchester and Kinderhook, NY: St. Jerome Publishing.

Sakamoto, R. (2011). 'Koreans, Go Home!' Internet nationalism in contemporary Japan as a digitally mediated subculture. *Asia-Pacific Journal: Japan Focus*. Retrieved January 10, 2021, from http://hdl.handle.net/2292/17431

Sakamoto, R., & Allen, M. (2007, October 4). Hating the Korean wave comic books: A sign of new nationalism in Japan? *Japan Focus*. Retrieved January 10, 2021, from www.japanfocus.org/-Mathew-Allen/2535

Sansom, G. (1958). *A history of Japan to 1334*. Stanford: Stanford University Press.

Schäffner, C. (1998). Skopos theory. In M. Baker and K. Malmkjaer (Eds.) (pp. 237–238), *Routledge Encyclopedia of Translation Studies*. London; New York: Routledge.

Schäffner, C. (2004). Political discourse analysis from the point of view of translation studies. *Journal of Language and Politics*, 3(1), 117–150).

Schäffner, C. (2012). Finding space under the umbrella: The Euro crisis, metaphors, and translation. *Journal of Specialised Translation*, 17(2).

Scott, C. (2012). *Literary translation and the rediscovery of reading*. Cambridge: Cambridge University Press.

Seoul Broadcasting System (SBS). (2005, July 29). 일본만화 "혐한류", 궤변 투성이 [Japanese manhwa "Kenkanryū", a load of sophistry], 8pm News report. Retrieved August 18, 2021, from http://news.naver.com/main/read.nhn?mode=LSD&mid=sec&sid1=115&oid=055&aid=0000050464

Seth, M. (2010). *A history of Korea: From antiquity to the present*. Hawaii, HI: Rowman and Littlefield Publishers.

Sharifian, F. (2009). Figurative language in international political discourse: The case of Iran. *Journal of Language and Politics*, 8(3), 416–432.

Shin, Y., Lee, H., Jeon S., Lee, M., Kim, S. H., Kim, H. G., Shin, G. M. (2006). 동아시아의 한류 (*East Asia's Korean Wave*) (pp. 14–19). Seoul: Jeonyaewon.

Song, A. (2007). 韓流ブーム/北朝鮮バッシング/嫌韓流　現象と、日本版ネオリベラル多文化主義の文化政治 [The phenomenon of the 'Hallyu boom'/'North Korea bashing'/'Hate Hallyu' and the 'cultural politics' of Japanese publishers' neoliberal 'multiculturalism']. In *Gendai no riron* (*Modern Theory*) (pp. 52–60). Tokyo: Akashi Shoten.

Spiegel Online. (2010). *The Kampf for 'Mein Kampf' – Annotated Version of Hitler's Polemic in the Works*. Retrieved July 15, 2021, from www.spiegel.de/international/germany/the-kampf-for-mein-kampf-annotated-version-of-hitler-polemic-in-the-works-a-676019.html

Sugiura, M. (2006). 表現行為における他者　嫌韓流の自家撞着 [The other within the act of expression – The self-contradiction of 'Kenkanryū']. *Geibunkō, 11*, 61–74.

Sugiura, M. (2007). 嫌韓流は如何なる蒙を啓くのか?　［含　座長コメント］ [What kind of enlightenment does 'Kenkanryū' provide? (with comments from the chairperson)]. In *Manga Kenkyū* (*Manga Research*) (pp. 25–33). Tokyo: Japan Society for Studies in Cartoons and Comics.

Swope, K. (2006). Beyond turtleboats: Siege accounts from Toyotomi Hideyoshi's second invasion of Korea, 1597–1598. *Sungkyun Journal of East Asian Studies, 6*(2), 177–206.

Swope, K. (2015). Ming grand strategy and the intervention in Korea. In J. Lewis (Ed.), *The East Asian War, 1592–1598: International relations, violence and memory* (pp. 162–169). London: Routledge.

The Guardian. (2015). *British Jews give wary approval to the return of Hitler's Mein Kampf*. Retrieved January 10, 2021, from www.theguardian.com/world/2015/dec/26/hitler-main-kampf-wary-welcome-british-jews

The Guardian. (2016). *High demand for reprint of Hitler's Mein Kampf takes publishers by surprise*. Retrieved January 10, 2021, from www.theguardian.com/world/2016/jan/08/copies-of-hitlers-mein-kampf-go-on-sale-in-germany-for-first-time-in-70-years

Toury, G. (1995). *Descriptive translation studies – and beyond*. Amsterdam and Philadelphia, PA: John Benjamins.

Turnbull, S. (2003). *Fighting ships of the far east (2): Japan and Korea AD 612–1639*. Oxford: Osprey Publishing.

Tymoczko, M. (2000). Translation and political engagement: Activism, social change and the role of translation in geopolitical shifts. *The Translator, 6*(1), 23–47.

Tymoczko, M. (2014). *Enlarging translation, empowering translators*. Manchester and Kinderhook, NY: Routledge.

United Nations. (2018). *Treaty on basic relations between Japan and Republic of Korea (1965)*. Retrieved July 20, 2021 from https://treaties.un.org/doc/Publication/UNTS/Volume%20583/volume-583-I-8471-English.pdf

van den Broeck, R. (1978). The concept of equivalence in translation theory: Some critical reflections. In J. S. Holmes, J. Lambert, & R. van den Broeck (Eds.), *Literature and translation* (pp. 29–47). Leuven: Academic.

van Doorslaer, L. (2007). Risking conceptual maps. In Y. Gambier & L. van Doorslaer (Eds.), *The metalanguage of translation*. Special Issue of Target. Target International Journal of Translation Studies. (Vol. 19, Issue 2, pp. 217–233). Amsterdam: John Benjamins.

Venuti, L. (Ed.). (1992). *Rethinking translation: Discourse, subjectivity, ideology*. London and New York, NY: Routledge.

Venuti, L. (2003). Translating Derrida on translation: Relevance and disciplinary resistance. *The Yale Journal of Criticism, 16*(2).

Venuti, L. (2008). *The translator's invisibility: A history of translation*. London: Routledge. (Original work published 1995)

Vermeer, H. J. (1989). *Skopos and commission in translation action* (L. Venuti, Trans., pp. 227–240). (Originally work published 2004). London, New York: Routledge.

Vermeer, H. J. (1994). Translation today: Old and new problems. In M. Snell-Hornby, F. Pöchhacker, & K. Kaindl (Eds.), *Translation studies: An interdiscipline* (pp. 1–20). Amsterdam: John Benjamins Publishing.

Wada, H. (2011). 日本の戦後和解とアジア女性基金の努力 [Japan's post-war reconciliation and the Asian Women's Relief Fund efforts]. In K. Satō & N. Frei (Eds.), 過ぎ去らない過去と取り組み [*A past and struggle that will not pass*]. Tokyo: Iwanami Shoten.

Wada, H. (2012). 慰安婦問題二十年の明暗 [20 years of the comfort women problem in contrast]. シンポジウム 慰安婦問題の解決に向けて [*Towards a resolution to the comfort women problem – symposium*]. Tokyo: Shirazawasha.

Wang, G. H. (2009, May 21). 日만화 '혐한류' "화장실 낙서에 불과"[Japanese *manga* 'Hate Korean Wave' "No more than bathroom graffiti"]. *Yonhap News*. Retrieved August 7, 2021, from http://news.naver.com/main/read.nhn?mode=LSD&mid=sec&sid1=100&oid=001&aid=0002672093

Weiner, M. (1994). *Race and migration in imperial Japan*. London: Routledge.

Weisman, S. R. (1991). Japanese translator of Rushdie Book found slain. *The New York Times*. Retrieved May 5, 2021, from www.nytimes.com/books/99/04/18/specials/rushdie-translator.html

White, B., & Kaplan, E. (2006). *Kenkanryu Material Analysis*. Retrieved February 2, 2021 from http://oicdblog2.blogspot.com.au/2006/10/kankanryu-material-analysis.html

Wu, Y., & Shen, C. (2014). (Ir)reciprocal relation between text and paratext in the translation of Taiwan's concrete poetry: A case study of Chen Li. In V. Pellatt (Ed.), *Text, extratext, metatext and paratext in translation* (pp. 103–120). Newcastle upon Tyne: Cambridge Scholars Publishing.

Yalman, O. (1994, November). Burned: An author charged with inciting a crowd to kill him. *Columbia Journalism Review*. https://indexarticles.com/reference/columbia-journalism-review/an-author-charged-with-inciting-a-crowd-to-kill-him/

Yamano, S. (2005). マンガ嫌韓流 (*Hate Korean Wave*). Tokyo: Shinyusha Mook.

Yamano, S. (2006). マンガ嫌韓流2 (*Hate Korean Wave 2*) (pp. 254–255). Tokyo: Shinyusha Mook.

Yamano, S. (2009). マンガ嫌韓流4 (*Hate Korean Wave 4*). Tokyo: Shinyusha Mook.

Yamano, S. (n.d.). Retrieved June 6, 2021, from http://propellant.fc2web.com/index.html

Zanettin, F. (Ed.). (2008). *Comics in translation*. Manchester and Kinderhook, NY: St. Jerome Publishing.

Zitawi, J. (2008). Disney comics in Arab culture(s) – A pragmatic perspective. In F. Zanettin (Ed.), *Comics in translation* (pp. 152–171). Manchester and Kinderhook, NY: St. Jerome Publishing.

Zulawnik, A. (2016). Ken-honyaku-ryū: Issues in the Translation of Controversial Texts Focusing on the Manga Comics Hate Korean Wave and Hate Japanese Wave. In S. Pasfield-Neofitou & C. Sell (Eds.), *Manga vision* (pp. 227–250). Melbourne: Monash University Press.

Zulawnik, A. (2020). "Death to the translator!" – A case study on risk in translation. *The AALITRA Review: A Journal of Literary Translation, 15*, 6–23.

Index

Note: Page numbers in *italics* indicate figures and page numbers in **bold** indicate tables.

116   Index

van den Broeck, R. 40, 63
Venuti, L. 4, 16, 21, 23, 33
Vermeer, H. J. 16–17, 19
video games 22
visibility 3–4, 7, 18; *see also* translator
 visibility
visual metaphors: *manga* and 40, 49;
 translation of 3, 34, 40, 63, 65

Wakamono dorei jidai (Yamano) 8n2
wareware nippon-jin (us Japanese) 60
Winter Sonata (Digital Daijisen) 14
Winter Sonata (Fuyu no Sonata) 91
Winter Sonata (Gyeoul Yeonga) 91
World Jewish Congress 5

Yamano, Sharin **53**; on Hate
 hallyu/kanryū movement 6;
 Kenchūgokuryū 8n2; *Naruman!* 8n2;
 online publishing and 6; response
 to criticism 62–64, *64*; on South
 Korean popular culture 6; travel in
 South Korea 6–7; *Wakamono dorei*

jidai 8n2; *see also Manga Kenkanryū*
 (*Hate Hallyu: The Comic*) (Yamano);
 Manga Kenkanryū (*Hate Hallyu*)
 translation
yogu (*seeking*) 77
yōkyū (*seeking*) 77
Yonhap News Agency 7

zainichi chōsenjin (*North Korean
 origin*) 80
zainichi gaikokujin (*foreigners in
 Japan*) 81
zainichi kankokujin (*South Korean
 origin*) 80
zainichi Koreans 13, 80–82, 90
Zentrum fur Antisemitismusforschung
 (*Centre for Research on
 Antisemitism*) 5
Zhong, Zhang 95n5
Zulawnik method *see* Great Manga
 Application Onidzuka (GMAO);
 Manga Kenkanryū (*Hate Hallyu*)
 translation

For Product Safety Concerns and Information please contact our EU
representative GPSR@taylorandfrancis.com Taylor & Francis Verlag GmbH,
Kaufingerstraße 24, 80331 München, Germany

Printed and bound by CPI Group (UK) Ltd, Croydon, CR0 4YY
11/04/2025
01844010-0009